HIS RELIGION AND HERS

CLASSICS IN GENDER STUDIES

Series Editor Michael Kimmel
Dept. of Sociology, SUNY at Stony Brook

Each generation of scholars rediscovers the "classics" that it needs. These works ground our contemporary research and provide historical context. What makes them "classics" is not simply that they're old, but that they continue to speak to contemporary concerns. Sadly, many brilliant works by major scholars and thinkers that were so influential in their time have passed out of print. The books in this series will reintroduce these works both to established scholars and to a new generation of students and researchers as they examine the origins of our understanding of contemporary gender relations.

Books in the Series

The Home: Its Work and Influence, Charlotte Perkins Gilman (2002)
Reprint of the 1903 edition with an introduction by Michael S. Kimmel

Concerning Children, Charlotte Perkins Gilman (2003)
Reprint of the 1900 edition with an introduction by Michael S. Kimmel

His Religion and Hers: A Study of the Faith of Our Fathers and the Work of Our Mothers, Charlotte Perkins Gilman (2003)
Reprint of the 1923 edition with an introduction by Michael S. Kimmel

About the Series Editor

Michael S. Kimmel is professor of sociology at the State University of New York, Stony Brook. His publications include *The Politics of Manhood* (1996), *Manhood in America: A Cultural History* (1996), and *The Gendered Society* (2000). He is the current editor of the international, interdisciplinary journal *Men and Masculinities*.

Classics in Gender Studies Series
AltaMira Press
1630 North Main Street #367
Walnut Creek, CA 94596
(925) 938-7243
www.altamirapress.com

His Religion and Hers

*A Study of the Faith of Our Fathers
and the Work of Our Mothers*

CHARLOTTE PERKINS GILMAN

A REPRINT OF THE 1923 EDITION
WITH AN INTRODUCTION BY MICHAEL S. KIMMEL

ALTAMIRA
PRESS

A Division of
ROWMAN & LITTLEFIELD PUBLISHERS, INC.
Walnut Creek • Lanham • New York • Toronto • Oxford

AltaMira Press

A division of Rowman & Littlefield Publishers, Inc.
1630 North Main Street, #367
Walnut Creek, CA 94596
www.altamirapress.com

Rowman & Littlefield Publishers, Inc.
A wholly owned subsidary of The Rowman & Littlefield
Publishing Group, Inc.
4501 Forbes Boulevard, Suite 200
Lanham, MD 20706

PO Box 317
Oxford
OX2 9RU, UK

British Library Cataloguing in Publication Information Available

Library of Congress Cataloging-in-Publication Data

Gilman, Charlotte Perkins, 1860–1935.
    His religion and hers : a study of the faith of our fathers and the
work of our mothers / Charlotte Perkins Gilman ; with an introduction
by Michael S. Kimmel.
        p.   cm.—(Classics in gender studies)
    Originally published: New York : Century, 1923.
    Includes bibliographical references.
    ISBN 0-7591-0386-0 (cloth : alk. paper)—0-7591-0387-9
(pbk. : alk. paper)
    1. Implicit religion.   2. Feminist theology.   3. Feminism—
Religious aspects—Christianity.   4. Sex role.   I. Title.   II. Series.

BL98.7 .G55   2003   2003018400
202'.082—dc22

Printed in the United States of America

The paper used in this publication meets the minimum requirements of
American National Standard for Information Sciences—Permanence of
Paper for Printed Library Materials, ANSI/NISO Z39.48–1992.

CONTENTS

v

CONTENTS

CONTENTS

PREFACE

The human race has overcome most natural obstacles to its development. Insects and disease germs are our only extra-human enemies worth mentioning. Yet we still starve, suffer, and sin, and lead stunted, perverted lives—under no natural compulsion, merely owing to our own behavior.

Religion is the strongest modifying influence in our conscious behavior. It expresses our highest instincts, and serves, or should serve, our best advancement. Yet the religions of mankind, so far, are responsible for much evil as well as good, and the best we know have only brought us to our present state.

Women, as the race type, through the immeasurable power of social motherhood, should long since have developed a race far more intelligent, efficient, and well organized, living naturally at a much higher level of social progress.

Yet women, even in countries where artificial

obstacles have been removed, show few signs of appreciating the needs of the world, or their ability and responsibility for setting it right.

And religion, though in some instances developed far beyond its earlier limitations, is still held down by its primitive preoccupation with death and after-death, still fails in its application to life.   Our last great backsliding into warfare has failed to stir us to wiser living, only rousing anew that ancient fever of misplaced anxiety—death, death; and where is the dead man?

This book offers some light on certain artificial conditions that injure human life, and suggest a few changes that will improve it.

TWO

Man the hunter, Man the warrior,
Slew for gain and slew for safety,
Slew for rage, for sport, for glory—
    Slaughter was his breath;
So the man's mind, searching inward,
Saw in all one red reflection,
Filled the world with dark religions
    Built on Death.

Death, and the Fate of the Soul;—
The Soul, from the body dissevered,
Through the withering failure of age,
Through the horror and pain of disease,
Through raw wounds and destruction and fear;—
In fear, black fear of the dark,
Red fear of terrible gods,
Sent forth on its journey alone,
To eternity, fearful, unknown—
    Death, and the Fate of the Soul.

.   .   .   .

Woman, bearer; Woman, teacher;
Overflowing love and labor,

Service of the tireless mother
     Filling all the earth;—
Now her mind awakening, searching,
Sees a fair world young and growing,
Sees at last our real religion—
     Built on Birth.

Birth, and the Growth of the Soul;—
The Soul, in the body established,
In the ever-new beauty of childhood,
In the wonder of opening power,
Still learning, improving, achieving,
In hope, new knowledge, and light,
Sure faith in the world's fresh Spring,—
Together we live, we grow,
On the earth that we love and know—
     Birth, and the Growth of the Soul.

INTRODUCTION TO THE
ALTAMIRA PRESS EDITION

Charlotte Perkins Gilman made a career as an iconoclast. In her career as a feminist and a sociologist, in her books and magazine columns in *The Forerunner*, she had smashed some of our most sacred ideological assumptions—that the differences between women and men sprang from some innate, biological difference between male and female; that the home was a refuge from the strife and care of the workaday world; that maternal love and care was superior to care of children by strangers. In her fiction she explored the way that prevailing definitions of femininity literally drove women crazy, and how a society created and run entirely by women would be less bellicose (if less sexy) than the present one run by men.

His Religion and Hers, Gilman's last work, published in 1923, is certainly one of her bravest. Here she looks at organized religion through the same contrarian yet sensible feminist lens through which she had viewed economic, political and social life. Her concern is the consequences of religious ideas on people's everyday lives. She treats religious ideology as a secular ethics, as a guide for life. She is not in the least concerned with the "truth" of religious doctrine, but on its effects.

It was a book Gilman had been waiting her whole life to write. She was already a celebrated writer and thinker, widely read and discussed. Her breakthrough work, *Women and Economics* (1898) was a bestseller, and catapulted Gilman into the prestigious ranks of public intellectual—one whose works were as respected among scholars as they were influential among a larger public.

I.

She was born Charlotte Anna Perkins on July 3, 1860, in Hartford, Connecticut to one of the 19th century's most prominent families. Charlotte's father was a ne'er do well and a dilettante. He attended Yale but never graduated, studied law but never practiced, and abandoned the family soon after Charlotte's birth, returning only for occasional visits before the couple formally divorced in 1873. Never particularly feminine—she was physically strong, vigorous, and was passionate about sports—Charlotte first thought to be an artist, and entered the newly opened Rhode Island School of Design in 1878. Family problems intervened, and she left school without graduating; her early training, however, provided her with the basis to earn a living as a commercial artist.

Early in 1882, she met Charles Walter Stetson, a promising young artist in Providence. Their courtship was difficult and turbulent. Charlotte had resolved to remain single and devote herself to her career. Eventually, she capitulated to Walter's earnest courtship, and they were married in May 1884.

But Charlotte felt constantly torn. Marriage was a life or death struggle for women, tearing them between two irreconcilable passions—motherhood and career.[1] Charles may have been attentive, dutiful and even helped with the housework, but it could not resolve the tensions Charlotte felt, especially after the birth of her daughter, Katherine in March 1885. At first, Charlotte was overjoyed by motherhood, but she gradually sank into what she described as a "growing melancholia," a "constant dragging weariness miles below zero."[2]

Her emotional distress became increasingly acute. By 1887, Charlotte's depression had become so serious and debilitating that she sought the advice of Dr. S Weir Mitchell, the Philadelphia physician who had gained national fame for his treatment of a somewhat trendy, elite condition called "neuras-thenia." Mitchell saw neurasthenia—a nervous dis-order marked by both anxiety and depression—as a consequence of the overcivilized modern life, "that of the business man exhausted from too much work, and the society woman exhausted from too much play," as Charlotte described it.[3] In both cases, neurasthenia was marked by gender nonconformity. For men, that meant passivity and lassitude, derived from the sedentary effects of the modern workplace; for women, by contrast, neurasethenia was marked by depression over the balance between work and family, and the inability to function as properly fem-inine.

Mitchell's remedies returned to traditional gen-der norms and a strict separation of spheres. Mitchell told Charlotte to "Live as domestic a life as possible. Have your child with you all the time. Lie down an hour after each meal. Have but two hours intellectual life a day. And never touch a pen, brush, or pencil as long as you live." She tried. She "went home, followed those directions rigidly for months, and came perilously close to losing my mind."[4]

So, one day Charlotte got out of bed, took her daughter and left her husband, traveling first to

Pasadena and then to Oakland, California to live with her best friend, Grace Channing. Her diary entry reads: "Thirty years old. Made a wrong marriage—lots of people do. Am heavily damaged but not dead."

In California, Charlotte threw herself into work, and established her lifelong career as a writer and editor. Between 1888, when she left Walter Stetson to her death in 1935, Gilman published 8 novels, 171 short stories, 473 poems, and 1,472 nonfiction pieces—9 of them books.[5] In her *Forerunner* magazine alone, she wrote critical articles, editorials, essays, poetry, reviews, short fiction, and two serialized books a year; the full seven year run of the magazine equaled some 28 full-length books.[6] Yet prolific as she was, Gilman's writing turned on a few dominant themes: the transformation of marriage, the family and the home.

And even these returned insistently to her central argument, that "the economic independence and specialization of women as essential to the improvement of marriage, motherhood, domestic industry, and racial improvement."[7] The liberation of women—and of children and of men, for that matter—required getting women out of the house, both practically and ideologically. It was work that was "the normal life of every human being; work, which is joy and growth and service, without which one is a pauper and a parasite."

In 1898, Charlotte published *Women and Economics,* her breakthrough work of nonfiction, and perhaps her single greatest book. Subtitled "A Study of the Economic Relations Between Men and Women as a Factor in Social Evolution," the book was an immediate success, widely read and discussed both in the United States and abroad. The book, which *The Nation* called "the most significant utterance on the subject of women since Mill's *The Subjection of Women,*" established Charlotte as the leading intellectual in the American women's movement.

In this work, Gilman drew from several different sources to produce a groundbreaking and original synthesis. From Marx and others, she took the idea that the central arena of human life is the realm of production, and that the workplace was the site of both oppression and liberation. What's more she also agreed that the differences among people were not to be found in nature, in biological differences, but rather from the way they are raised.[8] But unlike Marx, who had limited his discussion to economic classes, Gilman applied the idea to gender. Women and men were far more alike than they are different, she argued, but they are socialized to be dramatically different and at a cost to both women and men. From Darwin, she took the idea of progress and evolution. We have changed, she observed, and thus we can change and we must change. A theory of evolution underlies all Gilman's work, from her critique of the home as an anachronistic throwback to her vision of a future of economic independence and professional housework and childcare. From Thorstein Veblen she took the blistering critique of woman as ornament, as a medium of exchange between men. And from the sociologist Lester Ward she took the idea that women, not men, were the originators of evolution, the origin of the species. Ward was, Gilman wrote, "quite the greatest man I have ever known" and his "gyneco-centric" theory she thought "the greatest single contribution to the world's thought since Evolution."⁹

A series of more detailed works followed. *The Home: Its Work and Influence* (1903), *Concerning Children* (1900), and *Human Work* (1904) all detailed the deleterious consequences for women, for children and, yes, even for men of the subjugation of women. It was the single problem from which all of our current distorted policies—bombs instead of babies, profits instead of people, materialism instead of maternalism, corporate greed instead of compassionate generosity—stemmed.

II.

In *His Religion and Hers* she tries to develop a secular ethics; by recourse to simple reason, she believes she can set religion right and make it something for people to believe in again—not so they may escape their present miseries in some mythic afterlife, but so that they may transform their lives in the present.

In a sense, her argument revolves around a moral question she dares to pose in the middle of the book—a question that few had ever thought to answer: why is it that "neither religion, morality, nor ethics has made us 'good'"?[10] Typically, theologians would point to human fallibility: no matter how the clergy had tried to steer us towards the path of God, we humans always seemed to manage to fall off the path. The fault, they claim, was in our imperfection.

In this book, though, Gilman turns the tables. It's not that we are so imperfect, but that the religion that has been foisted upon us has led us astray. In part, she argues, religion has focused on the wrong thing—life after death instead of life before death—because, stated most simply, men have been in charge of it. "Religion, our greatest help in conscious progress, has been injured by coming through the minds of men alone." This is, she is quick to point out, "not in any essential fault of the male of our race . . ."[11] It's not that men have done this deliberately, but this distortion of what religion *could* be, *should* be, is the inevitable byproduct of the great tragedy of our species—"the subjugation of the female."[12] Much of the book is spent detailing the calamitous consequences of what she believes is our original sin: "making a private servant of the mother of the race." From this "exquisite monstrosity" all else flows.[13]

Gilman contrasts two types of religion, and typically, locates the source of these two types of religion not in any essentialist notion of "males" and "females" and their different natures, but rather in a system of male domination that leads *both* women and men to overspecialize in their own domain and to therefore *become* utterly different species. To Gilman, women may now be from Venus and men from Mars, but we all started out as Earthlings. And it was only by stealth, strength, and deception that

Martians have convinced themselves, and Venusians, that Mars is the superior planet.

This difference is crucial: it is not that women and men are inherently different, but centuries of a sexual division of labor and gender inequality have made women and men different. "We have seen the development of the human race carried on almost exclusively by men."[14] Differently placed in social relations and unequally valued, men and women, it stands to reason, have developed a different social ethics. Religion, thus far, has been based only on "his" ethics. It is "his" religion.

"His" religion is preoccupied with death. Because men in prehistory were concerned with war and hunting, and competition among men, they developed a religion that revolves around the question "What is going to happen to me after I am dead?"[15]

This focus on the afterlife has the ironic effect of spending far more time in the past than in the present. The major postulate of all death-based religions is that "life here is only a necessary evil, a mere stepping stone to life elsewhere." The present world is the world of the fallen, the sinner; it is in the afterlife that we will be rewarded. God, in such a schema, is highly personalized, as God is the sole arbiter of who will enter paradise. It is God's grace that will "rescue a pitiful few from a ruined world."[16]

And what a vision of heaven! Characterized by a "naïve masculinity," heaven is a hypermasculine paradise. "Never a feminine paradise among them. Happy Hunting Grounds—no Happy Nursing grounds."[17]

The focus on the afterlife also distracts us from the here and now. "There is no more pathetic instance of our perverse misunderstanding of the essential truth of religion than our colossal mistake of Christianity," she wrote in 1916, "ignoring the life of Christ and fixing all their attention on His death."[18]

Death-based religion fosters what Gilman sees as an individualism without limits, a constant requirement to please God and therefore acquire enough merit to enter heaven. And the emphasis on the afterlife leads to a "posthumous egotism" that defies reason, asking us to believe "that life stops just because he is dead." (This comment was prefigured in a 1916 column in *Forerunner* in which she decries the "pathetic egotism" of the early Hebrews who believed that they were the chosen people, while "all the rest of the world airily waved aside as inferior.")[19]

Which enables death-based religions to carry out

wars with moral righteousness. "No peace can ever be maintained in a wholly male world," she writes. "No war could ever endure for long in a world of equal men and women."[20]

The organizational consequences of "his" religion were equally disastrous. Diverted from attending to life in the present, religious leaders built an organization entirely focused on policing others (and, secondarily, itself). The costs are staggering. First, our bodies and their natural impulses are distorted. Death-based religion can brook no pleasures in the present, and so, "exalting celibacy, has again been potent in enabling us to resist not only a natural impulse but an exaggerated one." Celibacy is an utterly crazy idea, "as if gluttony and indigestion proved that it was wrong to eat."[21]

Socially, obedience replaces education. "In a church which insists on infallible authority we naturally find less general education, less freedom of thought, and greater emphasis on maintaining the proper state of mind."[22]

And, finally, catastrophically, "his" religion also inverted the relations between women and men, and instituted "the guileless habit of blaming women for the sin and trouble of the world." Thus, "his" religion demands her obedience to him; it sanctified the domination of women by men. "Wives submit your-selves to your husbands" went the Pauline doctrine. "So she submitted, to our racial degradation; or re-belled, and was destroyed."[23]

Happily, Gilman argues, the new motherhood will not submit to this continued victim-blaming, the degradation of women and the diminution of her abilities. "Her" religion, yet to be born, will be different.

Because women experience childbirth and nurtur-ing of life, so their religion would be life-affirming. Such a "birth based religion" would pose a different framing question: "What must be done for the child who is born?"

In lieu of "posthumous egotism," "her" religion would substitute an "immediate altruism," since a birth-based religion is essentially altruistic, in serv-ice to the real human future, not the past:

From her great function, birth, with its long pe-riod of prevision, its climactic expression in bring-ing forth the child, its years of unselfish service with rich results, she would have apprehended God in a widely different view from that of man—a power promoting endless growth.[24]

It is the Great Mother—a somewhat mythic creation that stands as a foil to the cavalcade of priests and saints and superordinate males who have constructed "his" religious edifice—who is the real source of life, the origin of humanity. And the mother, Gilman writes, is, by virtue of her experience, altruistic: "She works, not to get but to give." And God? God is "within us" not "above us."[25]

III.

Gilman was proud of *His Religion and Hers*; she called it "rather a useful and timely work, treating of matters of both lasting and immediate importance—sex and religion." Critics were less enthusiastic, and the book received mixed reviews. Gilman attributed that to two things, her antipathy to Freudianism, which dominated intellectual circles—"my views on the sex question do not appeal at all to the Freudian complex of to-day"—and the continued domination of "his" religion, which seduces people to look heavenwards for their afterlife, rather than earthwards to their actual lives. People are simply not "satisfied with a presentation of religion as a help in our tremendous work of improving this world," she wrote, "what they want is hope of another world, with no work in it."[26]

As with all Gilman's works, one is treated to side-light comments that reveal a brilliantly sarcastic and yet zealously ethical mind at work. She is furiously anti-Freudian, attributing to him an argument that sex "dominates the sensations even of a nursing baby, whose satisfaction, even when it is being fed at the mother's breast, he calls 'sexual'! A species of biological blasphemy, this; an idea so revolting to a healthy mind as to cause nausea . . ."[27]

She offers tidy little epigrams that today's policy-makers would do well to heed, such as "Spend on the school and save on the prison." And she reveals a remarkably prescient environmentalism: "We in America rapidly and recklessly deforesting our rich country, are making the future life of our own descendents poorer and harder."[28]

And although she opposes racism and calls slavery a black spot on America, she also occasionally reveals an abiding racialist attitude, mostly directed towards recent immigrants, but also occasionally toward native-born people of color.[29] On matters of race, eugenics, and race-suicide, Gilman was hardly a progressive; in fact, coupled with her anti-Semitism, such ideas marred her vision significantly.

But her view of religion remains compelling, in part because it is so firmly based on the realities of people's lives and not some abstract visions of them as either holy and pure or morally decrepit. His religion has distracted us from all that is sublime in this world, and enabled us to turn our collective backs on the true purpose of religion: "to turn its sublime force to human betterment on earth."[30]

NOTES

1. See, for example, "On Advertising for Marriage" in *Alpha*, Vol. 2, and "The Answer" in *Woman's Journal*, volume XVII, Number 40, October 2, 1886.

2. Charlotte Perkins Gilman, *The Living of Charlotte Perkins Gilman*, (New York: Harper and Row, 1975) 90, 91.

3. *The Living*, 95.

4. *The Living*, 96.

5. Gary Scharnhorst, *Charlotte Perkins Gilman: A Bibliography* (Metuchen, N.J.: Scarecrow Press, 1985).

6. *Herland*, Ann Lane, ed. (New York: Pantheon, 1979), vi.

7. *The Living*, 186.

8. Marx's famous epigram that "men make their own history," was echoed in his most famous articulation of this social constructionist position, in the Preface to his 1859 *Contribution to the Critique of Political Economy*, where he writes that "it is not the consciousness of men that determines their being, but, on the contrary, their being which determines their consciousness."

9. *The Living*, 187.

10. Charlotte Perkins Gilman, *His Religion and Hers*, (New York: Century, 1923), 154.

11. *His Religion*, 202.

12. *His Religion*, 206.

13. *His Religion*, 217, 237.

14. *His Religion*, 62.

15. *His Religion*, 46.

16. *His Religion*, 194, 247.

17. *His Religion*, 20.

18. *His Religion*, 18; "To My Real Readers" in *The Forerunner*, #7, December, 1916, 327.

19. "To My Real Readers," 326.

20. *His Religion*, 259.

21. *His Religion*, 180, 125.

22. *His Religion*, 225.

23. *His Religion*, 75, 246.

24. *His Religion*, 46, 247.

25. *His Religion*, 255, 292.

26. *The Living*, 327.

27. *The Living*, 165.
28. *The Living*, 171, 24.
29. *The Living*, 36.
30. *The Living*, 9.

HIS RELIGION AND HERS

HIS RELIGION AND HERS

CHAPTER I

INTRODUCTORY

HERE is a man weighing one hundred and fifty pounds, and here is a boulder weighing a ton. Can the man move the boulder? No.

Give him a long iron bar and another, smaller, stone—can the man move the boulder? Yes.

The boulder is no lighter and the man is no stronger, but by using the physical law of leverage the man can do what he cannot.

Here is a world in which genus *Homo* is the dominant race. It is the most wise, powerful, loving, skilful of all creatures. Has it made for itself a happy, prosperous, comfortable, smoothly progressive world? It has not. Yet "the world" of mankind is largely of our own making, is the result of our own behavior.

Can we govern our own behavior? Apparently not. We seem to be comparatively helpless transmitters of inherited impulses, and submitters to manufactured conditions.

Yet under the light and power of an idea, a concept, a theory, we can and do resist our impulses, change our conditions, alter our conduct beyond recognition. A concept is stronger than a fact.

This is the leverage by which the will of man can move mountains.

Under the influence of some cherished religious theory we have shown ourselves capable of resisting the deepest natural impulses, the hardest pressure of conditions. This is incontrovertibly shown by the ascetics and martyrs of all history. Such governing concepts need not even be true; men have cheerfully died for all manner of contradictory faiths.

Since the happiness and progress of man depend so much on his own behavior, since he is able to control his behavior under the influence of his ideas, and since his behavior remains so bad, it would appear that his ideas are largely wrong.

The most powerful group of concepts governing conduct are those forming a religion. Here is a lever to move the world.

If a religion is based on fact, and urges conduct in line with the natural laws of social evolution, it is the greatest help in our development. If it rests on false assumptions, forces into the mind illogical and contradictory deductions, and urges conduct which interferes with right progress, or which is quite useless, its tremendous power keeps us down instead of lifting us up.

To judge and measure religious doctrines, we must have some wider knowledge than that of the ancients. To criticize the basic assumptions of a religion, we must have in mind other assumptions, based on fact.

The assumptions underlying this study are these:

That humanity is an organic relationship of human beings;

That it is in process of evolution, social evolution;

That such social evolution is in line with natural law, and is to be greatly promoted by our conscious behavior, or greatly hindered and perverted;

That man is the only creature constructing his own environment, both physical and mental: he makes that which makes him;

That it is easily within our power to make this world such an environment as should conduce to the development of a noble race, rapidly and surely improving from generation to generation, and so naturally producing better conduct;

That our pitiful failures are due to an unnecessary ignorance, and to certain misconceptions, notably those of religion;

That the most widely entertained religious misconceptions rest on a morbid preoccupation with death and "another world";

That this is mainly due to the fact that they have been introduced and developed by one sex only, the male, in whose life as a hunter and fighter death was the impressive crisis;

That the female, the impressive crisis of whose life is birth, has an essentially different outlook, much more in line with social progress;

That a normal feminine influence in recasting our religious assumptions will do more than any

other one thing to improve the world; and that
no truth, in any religion, will be controverted by
such natural development.

Such a study will involve a presentation of the
sex characters as distinct from and subordinate
to race characters, and of the effect of sex on
religion; an analysis of some of the influences
which most modify conduct, and of our power of
self-determination as shown in morals, ethics,
philosophy, and religion.

It must clearly show what the female influence
would have been, is, and will be, when really active in the world; with a view of our present op-
portunities and powers, our easy ability to make
this world a place of joy and safety, of happy
exertion and unmeasured progress.

It should be definitely understood that no denial is made of the future life of the individual
soul after death; but that exception is taken to
our disproportionate interest in that prospect, to
the neglect of the future life of the race on earth.

It should be understood further that no invidious distinction is intended between the sexes;
no personal blame for men, who have made the

human world we live in, and such progress as we have achieved; and certainly no over-praise for the women men have made.

In the range of sex-distinction the female is superior; she, more than the male, is the race type; but in human distinction the female of our species is at present markedly inferior to the male. She is retarded by thousands of years of restriction, is seldom his equal in those processes which maintain social life and conduce to its progress; and, even as a female, does not fully exercise her primal powers nor fulfil her primal duties.

Her human capacities are by nature equal to his, but they have atrophied through long suppression, and her great power as selector of the best male for race-improvement, has been abrogated by her economic dependence upon him. As a mother, her influence has been limited by isolation and pitifully lowered by her position as domestic servant.

The "feminist revolt" of the last century was mainly against pressing personal injustice, and the enthusiasm of woman's new freedom seems, so far, to point more toward a distinctly masculine "self-expression" than to a feminine sense of duty to the race.

It is by no means generally realized by women that their true sex purpose is race-improvement; that their influence upon religion should be to turn its sublime force to human betterment on earth; that they have it in their power swiftly and strongly to push forward this so long-neglected world.

The main line of race-improvement is through the child.

The human mother fails in her full duty to the child because of her unnatural position as servant to the man.

Somewhere in the voluminous writings of that great social servant H. G. Wells, their author says something to this effect: Suppose the wisest men in the world were gathered together in a great hall to decide on what was most needed for human benefit, and suppose that into that hall came pouring, through a chute, babies at the rate of thirty a minute. Would anything be discussed there except what to do with those babies?

This rushing flood of babies, he pursues, is what is going on in the world, yet as a preëminent race problem we ignore it.

If we once admit that our life here is for the purpose of race-improvement, then we question any religion which does not improve the race, or the main force of which evaporates, as it were, directing our best efforts toward the sky.

This is not a controversial work about articles of faith. It does not contradict nor assert as to anything of which we have no knowledge. It deals with plain facts of this life, placing them in new relation and showing new connections and important consequences.

Improvement in the human race is not accomplished by extracting any number of souls and placing them in heaven, or elsewhere. It must be established on earth, either through achievement in social service, or through better children. There need be no quarrel over "the transmissibility of acquired traits"; whether the traits are "acquired" or appear through "the tendency to vary," appear they do and transmitted they are. This race, like others, is gradually modified and developed through heredity and environment.

It is here we face the peculiar failure of our race to progress as it should, owing to such persistent misbehavior as has led to the assumption of inherent wickedness. The progress we have made often seems to interfere with the relentless processes of nature, the "elimination of the unfit"; yet we have not substituted our own superior power of selecting the fit and making them fitter through education and environment.

Gains we have made, in many lines, most conspicuously in the vast development of machinery and applied power, but not in the stock.

In the major line of social duty, race-improvement, religion fails to guide. Our world, we are told, is a "fallen" world, or it is in a flux of endless personal transmigration. Nowhere does this greatest of human forces stand forth with: "The first duty of man is to improve the human race!"

Recognition of that fact and legitimate efforts to fulfil that duty, are wholly in line with the truth of any religion.

Though seven heavens stretch before us after

death, our duty, while we are alive, is to carry out on earth the divine purpose, the upbuilding of a noble humanity.

This fully seen, and our limitless power of fulfilment understood, there will be lifted from the human mind a crushing mountain of misconception. That "race-inferiority complex" which has paralyzed our conscious progress will be broken up.

The remote, uncertain, contradictory views concerning a book-derived God, which have been so often shaken when the world went more wrong than usual, will be replaced by the vital recognition of a most present and practical Force, working through us, and delayed in results not by a supposititious devil but by our own needless stupidity.

We grovel and "worship" and pray God to do what we ourselves ought to have done a thousand years ago, and can do now, as soon as we choose. There is nothing, absolutely nothing to prevent an intelligent organized race from making this world something we could be happy in and proud of. That we are not an intelligent organized race is our own fault, not God's nor the devil's.

A sense of social responsibility, a social conscience, hope and purpose for society, knowledge of the laws of social evolution, lives governed and guided in accordance with those laws—these are what we need.

To our unused and long-discouraged minds the teaching of world-improvement seems a cold, intangible theory, whereas it is a most practical, immediate prospect, and of limitless enjoyment in attainment.

We have to stretch our minds, it is true, but not beyond their natural range. We are human, and humanity is a collective form of life. Its constituents, as human beings, have the collective instincts and abilities. But all these human faculties are cramped and twisted, stiff with long disuse, and heavily encrusted with old lies.

Sunk in personality, grossly preoccupied with over-developed sex and all its accompanying self-indulgences, **ignorant** of sociology and without the help of a life-promoting religion, we blunder on as best we may. So pitifully slow is our development that the necessary inquiries demanded by the last war showed proud America that a large proportion of her children were morons. Morons. Half-wits and quarter-wits. The mentality of a child of twelve in grown men and women.

What are the mothers of the race doing, that they should breed morons for citizens?

What have the fathers of the race done, that the minds and bodies of the people are weakened and corrupted?

What is religion contributing, that we care so much about the possible loss or gain to our own precious souls, and care nothing for the inevitable loss or gain of the world?

We who are able to stretch our minds backward to the beginnings of the earth, upward into the measureless reaches of astronomy, onward into a vision of eternity for our personal souls; we who look back through history into anthropology, and back of that into zoölogy, and back of that into geology—let us take heart of grace and look forward in sociology for a few generations.

By understanding the laws of health and enforcing them through right physical education and environment—nothing more severe than that —we can fill the world with such bodies as were reared in Greece when Greece was young. We can train minds as able to think clearly as they are to act strongly on their own decisions. We can cultivate a social consciousness in which a wise and vivid patriotism, a patriotism which means life-service, will be dominant over primitive instincts based on the ties of blood. We can make the earth safer, more beautiful, increasingly fertile, and build cities lovely and clean.

The enormous wealth already within our power to make we·can multiply and distribute until no child need suffer from improper environment.

An organized world, established peace, universal education of a far higher order than we now know, and a development of the individual which will make us look back on our present abilities with pity and shame—these things we can have for the making.

To such proposals there is no large response. Some "returned spirit" muttering vaguely of future happiness in another world means more to us than all the present and coming happiness which is not only our right but our duty here.

It is toward such immediately beginning and progressive happiness, such noble yet simple duty that these suggestions as to sex and religion are offered.

CHAPTER II

MAN'S interest in something beyond the present is undeniable, and is, in its higher forms, peculiar to himself.

It is true that many of our zoölogical inferiors provide by a blind instinct for the advantage of the next generation, and that some of them seem intelligently to foresee the deprivations of the coming winter, arranging for food and shelter during its rigors.

But this short-range and purely practical provision is nothing compared with our limitless and spiritual prevision. We do, indeed, like the mud-wasp, lay up supplies for our children, and buy coal in April,—if we can afford it,—but belief in these matters merits no martyrdom. The faith we passionately uphold is in what we call life after death, "the great beyond."

That life goes on after death is clear; no one is so fondly egotistical as to assume that life stops just because he is dead.   Human life, with all its adventures and misadventures, has been going on for a long time, and shows no signs of stopping. This, however, is not the point of interest.   It is not the undeniable "beyond" of our life here, but that of our life somewhere else about which each is excited.   The beyond, for the individual, after his death, is the key-note of most of our great religions.   Neither the individual nor the religion thinks or cares about the beyond of human life on earth.

The general interest of humanity in the future life seems to rank almost as a race instinct.   As such it might be held to indicate, in our social consciousness, a dim prevision of improvement, a sort of psychic recognition of social evolution.   It has not been so understood, but is held to prove some other life, knowledge of which will guide our conduct in this one.

The earthly paradise of a Promised Land, flowing with milk and honey, assured to them and their children in this life, was no more compelling a spur to action to the early Hebrews than was the hoped-for Valhalla, flowing with beer and bloodshed, to early Teutonic peoples. No future life offered has been more practically popular than that of the Moslem. When he died, most particularly when he died in battle for his faith, he went directly to a scene of bliss which any man was quite competent to enjoy, an eternity of feasting and dalliance with ladies of imperishable youth and beauty.

While considering the attractions of the various beyonds as set forth in one religion after another, recognition is due to what is absolutely the most prodigious prize ever offered the human soul, the dazzling future of the good Mormon.

The God worshipped by Jew, Christian, and Moslem, Mormons esteem to be the especial deity of this earth and its people, who are literally his children through Adam; the universe full of countless inhabitable earths, and to each earth its god. To these illimitable worlds will come in time their deities, recruited from the ranks of Latter-day Saints. The perfected Mormon soul, in the fullness of time, becomes God; not resolved into an Infinite Being, as believes the humbler Buddhist, but a quite separate divinity, all by himself. There is a delicious Americanism in this idea. Not only may any little boy be President, but he may be God.

A rather conspicuous point to be noted in all these joy-promising futures is their naïve masculinity. Never a feminine paradise among them. Happy Hunting-Grounds—no happy Nursing-Grounds. No seductively mustached he houris, eternally gallant and devoted, beckon to pious lady Moslems. It is the man Mormon who soars to divinity; the women, in indefinite numbers, may also soar if properly married to him, but their position is distinctly subordinate, as here.

The Christian heaven is as appealing to women as any; but if that decoratively imaged city of golden streets and pearly gates, with its later envisaged choirs of angels with harp and crown, does please them more, it seems on the other hand less attractive to men. No man can rush to death in battle as much stimulated by the hope of a harp as of a houri.

With us the beyond which has had the most force is not heaven but hell. Any study of old sermons shows this in overwhelming proportion.

We were told that heaven was our home, to be sure, and in truth it was shown most desirably contrasted with the alternative, but little eloquence was spent in depicting its allurements compared with the fervid orations on the terrors of hell.

Times change; habits change; even human nature, usually advanced as the type of immutability, changes, and with these have changed our precise ideas about the still-desired beyond. On what, as a matter of fact do these ideas depend? On three sources—revelation, imagination, and information, all of which vary. Every religion has its revelations, and even within a religion revelations do not always agree.

If there are any who question this, still holding that every word of our Scripture is true, and none contradictory of another, let them be referred to Ecclesiastes iii, 19 and 20, on this very topic:

For that which befalleth the sons of men befalleth beasts; even one thing befalleth them: as the one dieth, so dieth the other; yea, they have all one breath; so that a man hath no preeminence above a beast; for all is vanity.

The Preacher was in a gloomy mood and felt as he spoke, but few of us believe that what he felt was true.

Imagination has had a greater share in our general beliefs about the beyond than we are commonly aware. Dante and Milton are responsible for most of our views on the subject. The fluent sermonizer and pious hymn-maker have added their contributions. Many of our popular beliefs find their only base in these imaginings.

Then comes information, at present the most accepted source. During all the ages, under the heaviest pressure of revealed religion and in spite of the best efforts of imagination, we have always been intrigued by the idea of direct communication with some one who had been there. So many went,—all of us, in fact, as time passed,— it did seem as if they might get word to us. Never has this feeling been stronger than now. Revelation does not bind as it did, imagination is too easy; we want the facts from eye-witnesses.

So the modern world, with its popular education, its scientific training, its laboratory methods and what not, is now eagerly receiving reports from those "on the other side."

Even here we do not find agreement.   It seems virtually impossible to gather any clear and convincing impression as to what awaits us in this beyond, the personal life after death.

How about the other beyond, the human life after our death, here, which we all know does go on, such as it is?   There are marked points of difference between this beyond and the spiritual. For one thing, it is finite, a little period, variously estimated among the hundreds or thousands of millions of years; we are more attracted by the idea of eternity.   An odd preference, this, because in this life we soon weary of anything that lasts too long, but so it is.

Neither does the earthly beyond have the unchangeable character of the eternal one, but it has altered continuously from its beginning, each age modifying the future for the next.   It is usually believed that by careful conduct we may affect our position in the future life, but we may not change its conditions.   Whereas the future conditions of all who follow us on earth it is within our power to change, for better or for worse.

In those portions of the earth's surface which have been completely deforested by previous occupants, the future life of all later ones has been made more difficult. We in America, rapidly and recklessly deforesting our rich country, are making the future life of our own descendants poorer and harder.

Those who have contributed to mankind the accumulated discoveries and inventions, the accruing knowledge and skill, the lasting works of use and beauty, have improved the future life of each following generation. For the most part it has been done unwittingly, for advantage in the present life rather than a desire to improve the future, but the benefit remains.

Our personal interest in a future life on earth has been shown mainly in the wish to be remembered, by the most meager gravestone or the pyramid of Cheops. By means of hospital beds, memorial windows, or other name-labeled endowments and bequests we seek to linger in the minds of our fellows, and sometimes we are "immortalized" by poet or sculptor. Undying fame is a dear ambition, though seldom realized.

"They have ceased, but their glory shall never cease,
Nor their light be quenched in the light of peace,

For the rush of their charge is resounding still
That saved the army at Chancellorsville."

The desire to insure some persistence of the individual life in an earthly beyond, involves no interest in the life of other people. It is a fairly common sentiment, but by no means so compelling as concern for the unearthly one; the wish to live in the minds of our fellows bears no comparison to the wish to live, eternally, somewhere else.

There rises an odd confusion on this point among those who consider life to be exclusively in mind rather than in matter, which is clearly illustrated in the following instance.

It was once my fortune in a boarding-house, where a hasty wooden partition and thin door between my room and the next gave no vocal privacy to either occupant, to learn much of the methods of my neighbor, who received callers both professionally and socially. One day he was consulted by a fellow-believer, who regarded him as more advanced and wished to be strengthened in the faith.

"When I—pass on," he said earnestly, "nothing is lost, all that is real is in the mind, goes with me in the mind?"

The higher authority assured him that this was so.

"I do not lose my wife and children," pursued the seeker; "they exist in my mind, they go with me in my mind, I have not left them."

"True," agreed his comforter; "you are quite right."

"Then," came the intense climax, "why should I keep up that life-insurance?"

This seems a reasonable question, if one follows the argument closely. But the authority was a man of practical sense as well as spiritual faith.

"Wait a moment," he urged. "Does your wife share your belief in this matter?"

The questioner considered, and candor compelled him to admit that his wife, in such case, might entertain a haunting conviction that she was still existent, a widow, with children to support.

"So long as she feels that way," he was then instructed, "you had better keep up your insurance."

Some there have been, from age to age, who were keenly interested in our earthly future, and saw in it tremendous possibilities for human happiness. Books have been written on the subject, alluring pictures drawn, like those of heaven, and occasionally, as in Wells's "Time Machine," suggestions made of something very like an earthly hell.

For ideas on this future we have but one of the three sources that supply the other. There is no revelation as to our coming life here, and no information. No one can even pretend to come back and tell us about it, except in books. These books, from Plato to Bellamy, and Wells himself, fail to agree in detail. Mr. Wells's books, indeed, do not even agree with one another. And since they all assume as a principle that people are going to behave differently from their present habits, we have never found them convincing. Yet this difference in behavior is also assumed in descriptions of our heavenly future; indeed, even those who come back to tell us about it are hardly recognizable for what they were, without discouraging us about heaven.

If religion had concerned itself with our

earthly future, it would have had a strong influence. Such pictures as it has given us of a vague millennium have been, if anything, less convincing than the Utopias. We can more easily believe in people's behaving well toward one another—as, indeed, many of them do now—than in contiguous naps of lions and lambs. The most frequent assumption of religion regarding our earthly future (I speak here of the Christian religion) is that we shall go from bad to worse and end in total destruction—except of course in the case of those who have handled this life with an eye single to their personal interest in another one, or, in a still narrower view, of a mere handful arbitrarily "elected." This is clearly a misnomer; it should have been "selected"; there was, surely, no vote taken upon members of either the upper or the lower house!

Yet if we lack revelation and information on this really important beyond, we have one base the other lacks—facts to build on. This practical future of ours has been in the building for a long time, quite long enough to show clearly what behavior it is which makes the lives of those who follow it better or worse.

In the one matter of health, a condition which we all admit is desirable, if our ancestors, thoughtful of the future, had so lived that we were all strong and well, that future, now our present, would be far more agreeable. Admitting that these ancestors did not know how, and struggling manfully to overcome the plagues they have left us, we have this comfort: we do know how to eliminate from our children's future, and from the continuing generations after them, some of the worst of our diseases.

Look, for instance, at that most unpleasant group of what we sagaciously call "social" diseases, they being due solely to personal misconduct, freely recognized as misconduct even by those who so misconduct themselves. The grievous affliction could be halted in its tracks in one generation, and wiped out in a few more.

No research, as for the cause of cancer, is needed; we know the cause. No study to discover the means of transmission is needed; we know the means. No insidious insect must be screened from our homes, and slain in its myriad infancy by wide-spread kerosene. It is wholly a matter of behavior, and quite within our power to check.

The trouble is that those heavily modifying forces, religion, law, custom, and public opinion, have never concerned themselves with this hand-made future of ours; the real, solid, unavoidable future which comes rolling down the ages toward us,—sure to come but ours to mold as we prefer,—hell, heaven, or the confused mixture we call human life and are so discouraged about.

There is inspiration in thinking that the earthly future is for children to be born into, while the other is for our own elderly souls, of which some of us are already tired and some frankly ashamed. The unconscious happiness of children, their swift development, their easy acceptance of all lovely surroundings, make it a pleasure to provide for them. Surely fathers, not to speak of mothers, should be more concerned about what will happen to their living children in the world we are making, than about what may happen to themselves after they are dead!

Our behavior as it affects other people has not been taken seriously enough by religion. After all, it is comparatively a small affair what happens to a single soul, no matter how eternally, compared with what is done to the world. Yet we go on, reaping what our ancestors have sown and sowing for our descendants to reap, as unconcernedly as if we really had no responsibility except in securing our own personal advantage. Furthermore, if religion would be clear and strong on the subject, it becomes plain that the very behavior which builds the best future for our descendants in this life, is conducive to our chances of happiness in the next, whereas the special rites and ceremonies which we were told would benefit us are of no possible benefit to our children.

Perhaps the other-life future is more attractive to us because it is more easily attained. One may be helped in. Methods vary according to different faiths, but most of them are elastic. A person may "sin" in some ways and make up for it in others; or, no matter how much a sinner, he may be forgiven at the last minute, and find his future unimpaired by his behavior. Not so here.

The earthly future, bright though it shines as something within our power to make, has its gloomy side. There is no "forgiveness" in the transmission of sins from father to son. The erring father, spiritually forgiven, may live in heaven as happy as a grig, but the innocent child, inheriting the future his father made, lives on earth in misery. We are so long-sighted in our passionate desire for an eternal existence in the other life, so short-sighted in our indifference to the really respectable number of millions of years before us in this one!

If only religion could be brought to take an interest in this earthly future, what a help it would be! Think of the hymns chanting tunefully of the beautiful life just before us, so easily ours to make. Think of the pulpit eloquence, painting in words of penetrating force our splendid, never-ending opportunity to make our future life on earth worthy of the God we believe in. Think of the appeal to the less spiritual of us, to those who never did get enthusiastic about eternity, or care so tenderly about their own souls, yet who could rise to the thought of improving this world for the children they love, and their children after them.

Then too, if this view were taken up by religion, it might affect public opinion, and perhaps, in time, the law. Even governments held to such a standard would be kept more strictly to the path of far-sighted economy and steady provision for the public good.

Private'y, one's future in the other life is one's personal affair.

Publicly, our common future in this life is our common affair, a social responsibility. Little care we for that, as yet. Our general attitude is that of the pessimistic Preacher before quoted:

Wherefore I perceive that there is nothing better, than that a man should rejoice in his own works; for that is his portion: for who shall bring him to see what shall be after him?

CHAPTER III

SUGGESTED CAUSES

O URS is the only race that can lift itself by its boot-straps. Like other species, we are pushed by heredity, moved this way and that by the tendency to vary, relentlessly modified to environment. Unlike other species, we can not only adapt ourselves most rapidly to a changing environment but change it to meet our needs; we need not depend on finding or catching our food, we raise it.

Beyond these advantages comes the capacity of the human mind to observe and remember, to formulate ideas and act upon them. These are the boot-straps.

The environment most effective upon us is the social one; what we think and believe is more potent in modifying our behavior than any outside condition. Witness women wearing furs in August.

On this plane of self-modified growth, with all

the ability of our associated brains to serve us, with a race memory historically preserved and a world-wide acquaintance with all the failures and successes of mankind to profit by, it would seem as if our race might easily surpass all others in health, beauty, happiness, and virtue.

Instead of which, we see ourselves the sickest beast alive, the wickedest, the most foolish. We have so utterly accepted our disadvantages that we speak of "poor human nature" as if it were in some way inferior to the rest of nature; and as for this beautiful world, we call it a "vale of tears," and support its miseries in the hope of finding a better world after we are dead.

With all the light and leading of our various religions, there remains under them this peculiar indifference to human improvement, this transference of our highest efforts toward securing future happiness elsewhere.

The religion which urges most of real race-improvement is that of Jesus. He taught unmistakably of God in man, of heaven here, of worship expressed in the love and service of humanity. But our strange death-complex was too strong even for his teachings. What he taught us to pray and work for here, was ignored in our eagerness to get to heaven through his virtues.

In this twentieth century we have seen Christian Europe hating and fighting exactly as did heathen Europe in the past. Christian Germany has left a record which we may mildly term inconsistent with the Christian faith. Christian Ireland is a beautiful example of forgiveness, patience, and loving one another. Our own Christian nation maintained slavery after every other advanced people had outgrown it, and still stands black before the world in that most hideous of savage practices, the slow torturing to death of helpless prisoners, which we cover by the term "lynching."

The Christian religion has been taught for about twenty centuries, but it has not established connection with life. Its revivalists still make their passionate appeal on a basis of what is to happen to us after death.

How are we to account for this peculiar trend of the human mind? What influence, during the slow ages when religious thought was dawning among us, turned it away from all the vivid actualities of this world, to the glittering or terrible possibilities of another?

The death-basis for religion is so old, so deep, that we must look for its cause in our earliest beginnings, in that long, dark period of savagery which covers so extensive a proportion of human existence.

It has been pointed out that thought was roused in the primitive mind by the crises in life, rather than by regularly recurring events. A sunset would be as awful as an eclipse if it occurred as rarely.

What was the principal crisis in the life of primitive men?

Their occupation was in hunting and fighting. They lived mainly by killing other animals, either to eat or to avoid being eaten, and in addition to these indispensable activities they varied the excitement by killing one another. After the slow, patient hours of tracking, of lying in wait, the strenuous pursuit, the fierce combat, came the climax—death.

Death was the event, the purpose of his efforts,

the success, the glory. If he was the dead one, we cannot follow further; but if he triumphed and saw his "kill" before him, here was cause for thought. The death-crisis, coming as the crashing climax to the most intense activity, naturally focused his attention on the strange result. Here was something which had been alive and was dead; what had happened to it? The creature which had fled so swiftly or struggled so violently had now stopped. It did n't go any more. The body was there as before, but something had gone from it. What was it? Where had it gone? The mind of the killer pitched forward, as it were, along the road of the spirit which had fled.

Here we have a simple, an obvious explanation of our early interest in death. Life meanwhile went on as unconsciously with us as with any other animal. Why should we think about that? But death was something to celebrate, to be followed by feasting and rejoicing, something which redounded to the glory of the killer, who draped himself with scalps and bears' claws, trophies of conquest.

The feasting following the kill had further results not to be overlooked in a study of the ori-

gins of religion.   Men ate in those times with no
saving grace of Fletcherism, no Roman devices
for food-control.   They gorged themselves to re-
pletion; they slept heavily; and from distended
stomachs rose dreams which call for no Freudian
explanation—stark nightmares from gluttonous
indigestion.   Then did the victim rise again; the
fight came to a different end.   That which was
dead lived, larger and more awful, looming nearer
and more ferocious till the sleeper woke screaming.
Here we have the natural base not only for belief in ghosts, as Spencer and others have shown,
but for the fear of ghosts as well.

However unpleasant a dead man may be, he is
certainly harmless, save, indeed, for later results
on the health of the living; and ghosts, as far as
recorded, do not bite.   It is hard to account for
that peculiar sinking terror which the low-grade
mentality feels of such phenomena, unless we
recognize it as the well-known paralyzing fear
felt in nightmares.   To this day the nightmare-
dreams of childhood are often dominated by
savage beasts—man's earliest dread and danger.

Since we know that the savage period of our
race life was by far the longest part of it, it is

easy to see how deep and strong became the death-complex in the primitive mind. By the time that definite religious ideas could be formulated, their direction was irrevocably determined. No small effort will be required in the mind of to-day to change that direction.

Dreams called for interpretation, and there arose interpreters. In the interpretation of dreams and in speculations about death, the active, empty mind of the early medicine-man was in no way hampered by facts. Along both these avenues the busy brain could course like a hare, could go as far as it liked in any direction. There was nothing to stop it.

It is hard for us, whose imaginations are encumbered by some knowledge, to reconstruct that "first fine careless rapture" of early thinkers. Thinking is fun to a normal mind, like any other natural exercise, and those very ancient ancestors of ours had lively brains, with no ballast. They were so intrigued by thinking on subjects concerning which nobody knew anything, that they hardly cared for the more difficult topics of real life, wherein one's glad imaginings are so brutally interrupted by stubborn facts.

With some discovery of healing herbs or crude invention, the dream-interpreter merged into the medicine-man, and the medicine-man, in the course of time, became the priest. This functionary was of immense importance in social development. What mankind needed more than anything else was power to think deeply, broadly, clearly. The priest was the only man who had time to think, as a business. His was the best job life had to offer. He was safer than a king, who, for all his glory, often had to fight. The priest need neither fight nor work; he was fed by the faithful, who brought sacrifices. The delicate taste in butcher's meat shown in Levitical law indicates how particular he grew from long indulgence.

In one religion after another, as they appear and spread over the earth, we find the continuing imprint of that old death-complex. Natural death, coming to the aged in due season, would never have roused such fevered interest. But since the great religions of the world have one and all come down to us through the minds of men, and since the fighting male kept the world confronted with death of old and young, manufacturing widows and orphans with a lavish hand, this constant horror still monopolized the attention of religious thinkers.

The profound speculations of the highly developed brain of India, in Brahmanism, Buddhism, and other faiths; the fierce enthusiasm of the Moslem, the wide-spread efforts of the Christian, all have overestimated death and underestimated life.

The theory of transmigration makes "this life" merely a link in an endless chain. The Buddhist theory saw "this life" as a poor and painful thing, "the wheel of change," something to be escaped from.

Even the teaching of Jesus, heart-warming, truth-filled doctrine of "God in man," of "Thy kingdom come on earth," of worship in love and service, was soon swamped by the resurgence of the older death-idea, and became to most of its followers a mere short cut to the "other life."

There was never a religion that would have gone so far toward building the kingdom of God on earth as the teaching of Jesus; and never one more blackened by hideous theories of hell and damnation, by persecutions, tortures, and devastating wars.

Christians are but too ready to admit how far they fall short of the teachings of their Master, fondly attributing their shortcomings to the fact that their standards are so high; whereas the failure is due to the persistence of the same old death-complex, to the focusing of their hope and purpose on "the other life," with the gross neglect of this one.

Pursuing the evidence of dominant masculinity in the evolution of religions, we find another conspicuous proof—the guileless habit of blaming women for the sin and trouble of the world. One religion after another shows scorn of women, making no provision for their pleasure in heaven, sometimes denying that they have souls at all. That ultra-masculine attitude has been maintained even in Christianity, owing to the fundamental mistake of those who arranged its early forms, and who insisted on keeping it connected with the Hebrew religion. This was not surprising, since so many of the early Christians were, still earlier, Hebrews, and naturally wished to preserve their old hopes and promises while facing the dangers and hoping for the rewards of the new faith.

By so doing we have brought down the ages that highly masculine and unworthy legend of "the curse of Eve." The discreditable shoving off of responsibility upon the shoulders of "the woman thou gavest me" lasted so effectively among Scotch Presbyterians that strong objections were made by them to the administering of chloroform to women in labor, on the ground that the suffering of the pangs of childbirth was her "curse" for original sin. The curse seems all the more unwarrantable when we read in the story itself that it was before Eve was made that Adam was commanded not to eat of the tree. She certainly was not forbidden.

In the "sacred" books of other old religions we find still lower opinions of women, constant discrimination against them, unvarying evidence of the fact that all our early religious thought came to the world through the minds of men alone. It is true that in the most primitive ones there is clear indication of the lingering influence of women, as shown in the worship of mother goddesses. That persistence of reverence for mother and child, through all the ages of masculine predominence, is a comforting proof of the undying force of natural law. But, speaking broadly, it is the man's mind which has modified religious thought and dominated religious action.

What would have been the effect upon religion if it had come to us through the minds of women?

If we are to trace our engrossing interest in death to the constant fighting and killing of early man, to the fact that death was the crisis in his activities, the significant event, rousing him to thought, what other interest are we to look for in the life of woman? What crisis set her mind at work, and what would have been its influence on religion?

The business of primitive woman was to work and to bear children. Her work was regular and repetitive; save for the gradual budding of invention and blossoming of decoration, it had no climax. There was small excitement in this, no thrilling event.

Yet her life held one crisis more impressive, more arousing, far, than man's; her glory was in giving life, not in taking it.   To her the miracle, the stimulus to thought, was birth.

Had the religions of the world developed through her mind, they would have shown one deep, essential difference, the difference between birth and death.   The man was interested in one end of life, she in the other.   He was moved to faith, fear, and hope for the future; she to love and labor in the present.

To the death-based religion the main question is, "What is going to happen to me after I am dead?"—a posthumous egotism.

To the birth-based religion the main question is, "What must be done for the child who is born?"—an immediate altruism.

Woman was not given to bootless speculation as to where the new soul came from, because of the instant exigencies of its presence.   It had come, indeed, but in a small and feeble state, utterly dependent on her love and service.   With birth as the major crisis of life, awakening thought leads inevitably to that love and service, to defense and care and teaching, to all the labors that maintain and improve life.

The death-based religions have led to a limitless individualism, a demand for the eternal extension of personality. Such good conduct as they required was to placate the deity or to benefit one's self—to "acquire merit," as the Buddhist frankly puts it. The birth-based religion is necessarily and essentially altruistic, a forgetting of oneself for the good of the child, and tends to develop naturally into love and labor for the widening range of family, state, and world. The first leads our thoughts away from this world about which we know something, into another world about which we know nothing. The first is something to be believed. The second is something to be done.

Before we attempt to indicate the natural consequences of birth-based religion, it should be repeated that here is no denial of personal immortality, against which there is no proof. Neither is there any condemnation of the male sex as such—only of its excessive development and disproportionate influence upon social evolution. Nor are women, such as we see about us, overrated or held capable of suddenly producing a flood of new truth and wise direction.

The position is that the tendencies of motherhood are in line with social progress, while the tendencies of the male sex, though quite legitimate in the propagation of the species, are often inimical to its social progress. Even had man and woman grown and worked together, her influence would have been more toward peaceful industrial development, and his more toward competitive methods; and, during the long period of her suppression and his expansion, an ultra-masculinity has interfered with normal social evolution.

We may clearly observe the intrinsic and far-reaching difference resultant from the instant action following upon birth, as compared with the endless discussion following upon death. The person being dead, all that we could do was to invent cumbrous rites of burial or other disposal of "the remains," sometimes indulging in the measureless folly of making mummies, or constructing huge enduring monuments to "preserve his memory"—those pathetic memoranda of persons long forgotten. All this being accomplished, nothing remained but to weep and mourn for the departed, or—and this was the engrossing thing—to discuss what might have happened to him.

How different when birth is the great event! Instead of grief and mourning, there are joy and triumph. Instead of a precarious "memory," there is an assured hope. Instead of boundless discussion, swift, well-founded action for the good of the growing thing, for the good of the world.

The primitive woman would have felt only "the maternal instincts," like any other animal. Even now—so thoroughly has woman's development been arrested—to most women motherhood is only a personal affair. But had she been free to broaden and deepen in humanity, she would have grasped the broader implications of her great work. As a conscious human being of to-day she may see her distinctive process in its true nature, the constant evidence of race immortality.

Whatever may happen to us individually, after death, the race does not die. It goes on, well, strong, wise, happy, rich, and progressive; or sick, weak, foolish, miserable, poor, and reactionary, according to what previous individuals have done while alive.

Birth is the most important event we know.   It is the ceaseless, visible re-creation of an undying race.   Through it we see humanity as a growing, continuous thing, coming into our hands fresh and plastic, open to unmeasured improvement or to degradation and decay, according to the circumstances with which we surround it.

Birth-based religion would steadily hold before our eyes the vision of a splendid race, the duty of upbuilding it.   It would tell no story of old sins, of anguish and despair, of passionate pleading for forgiveness for the mischief we have made, but would offer always the sunrise of a fresh hope: "Here is a new baby.   Begin again!"

To the mother comes the apprehension of God as something coming; she sees his work, the newborn child, as visibly unfinished and calling for continuous service.   The first festival of her religion would be the Birth Day, with gifts and rejoicings, with glad thanksgiving for life.   In the man's religion, the demand for ever-watching love and care, is that of the child, always turning to its mother—

An infant crying in the night,
An infant crying for the light,
And with no language but a cry.

The mother, feeling in herself that love and
that care, pours them forth on man, her child.
Such recognition and expression of divine power
are better than "worship." You cannot worship
a force within you; the desire of the mother soul
is to give benefit rather than to receive it.

As the thought of God slowly unfolded in the
mind of woman, that great Power would have
been apprehended as the Life-giver, the Teacher,
the Provider, the Protector—not the proud, angry,
jealous, vengeful deity men have imagined. She
would have seen a God of Service, not a God of
Battles. It is no wonder that Christianity was
so eagerly adopted by woman. Here was a religion which made no degrading discrimination
against her, and the fulfilment of which called
for the essentially motherly attributes of love and
service.

Women have adhered to all previous religions,
of course, having no others; but the new teachings of Jesus were widely accepted by them and
widely spread through their efforts. They were

not, however, the interpreters, the disputers, the establishers of creeds. They did not gather together to decide whether or not men had souls. They did not devise the hideous idea of hell, the worst thought ever produced by the mind of man. It cannot be attributed to women any more than to Jesus that his wise, tender, practical teaching of right living was twisted and tortured into a theory of right dying.

Believing as they must the doctrines of gloom and terror forced upon them, and sharing in the foolish asceticism of the early Christians, we still find in religious associations of women their irrepressible tendency to love and service. It was not in nunneries that Benedictine and Chartreuse were concocted; we do not see pictures of fat nuns carousing in cellars. No, the convent turns naturally to the school, the sisters as naturally to nursing and teaching; and when, outside of religious orders, we see the first little organizations of women, these are charitable, educational, or to help the sick.

We all know, some of us to our cost, the reformatory impulse in woman. Her instinct for care, for training, for discipline, is a grievous thing if highly developed and focused on too small a group. This is sadly well known to many a man who has to live under the tutelage of his wife's mother after having escaped from his own. The entrance of women upon politics was most dreaded because of that reformatory tendency.

This essentially feminine impulse would have had a strong influence in molding religion, an influence lightened by that vision of a new-born, ever-growing race, open to constant improvement. We cannot improve a dead man; we can, a baby. The mother does not sit down among her mischievous brood and say, "Children are bad by nature," and, "We cannot legislate morality." (As if legislation were not for precisely that purpose!) She would not call the inevitable mistakes of childhood a "problem of evil."

For most of us, accustomed to women as they are, and not accustomed to visualize normal womanhood and distinguish it from the present man-made variety, it is not easy to see great hope in femininity. The rise of woman, groping upward through limitations and injustices, has not been recognized for the world-changing phenom-

enon it is. The kind of women bred **and**
trained through ages of masculine selection **are**
not such as one would trust the world to, unas-
sisted. These laborious house servants, contented
with their lot, or discontented but still in it; these
decorated darlings, taking everything men give
them without even a momentary idea of producing wealth equal to that which they consume;
these enthusiastic reformers of other people; these
reckless indulgers of themselves—are they the
hope of the world?

Now that they have in large measure reached
their goal of "equality with men,"—not real
equality in social development but equality in immediate conditions,—it is sickening to see so
many of the newly freed using their freedom in
a mere imitation of masculine vices. Yet just
that is to be expected from a subject class, suddenly released, and the release of women is the
swiftest movement in history. Within a lifetime they have covered steps of advancement that
took thousands of years to build.

This is why we so sorely need the lifting force
of religion to carry us over this discordant period.
It is hard for men; they are losing forever the

woman servant of the past.   It tears at the very roots of their world, which is built on subject women.   It is hard for women, too.   They have become accustomed to dependence and have developed more strength to endure evil conditions than to change them.

The woman's conscience runs narrow and deep: she is loyal to her husband even when it means treason to her children, and devoted to her own children with complete indifference to the children of the world.   She does not yet recognize that her loyalty is due first to the human race, then to the child of her body, and then to her husband.   We cannot expect wide understanding of economics or politics from a so long-subject class.

But in religion women have always stood side by side with men, when allowed.   They made just as good saints and martyrs.   They have always been, in our own faith, the easiest converts, the most numerous supporters of the church. Now, when the basis of their faith swings round from death to birth, and widening knowledge teaches them the facts of sex and sociology, they will see themselves not as the poor second thought created for "Adam's express company," but as the main line of evolution; they will recognize their major purpose as not sex service nor house service, but world-service—the carrying on and improving of the human race.

CHAPTER IV

SEX- AND RACE-CHARACTERS

IT was a man, so human as to be above sex-pride; so great as to see the advantage of the world above the privileges of sex; so strong as to uphold a new-seen truth squarely in the face of the previous belief of the whole world, who gave us the facts as to the real relation of the sexes and its development in sub-human species and our own.

Lester F. Ward, in his "Pure Sociology," in the impressive chapter on "Phylogenetic Forces," set before the world his "Gynecocentric Theory" as opposed to the "Androcentric Theory" previously accepted.

Next to the theory of evolution itself, this is the most important single percept in the history of thought. Evolution is the greatest of all, changing as it did our whole concept of life; but this stands next in its value to humanity, as showing the greatest obstacle to social progress—the inverted relation of the sexes.

The book was published in 1903, and among the reviews of it, as its publishers collected them, not one recognized the epoch-marking nature of the new theory. The great "Woman-Suffrage" leaders of the time were not impressed by it. It fell into the sea of human thought apparently without causing a ripple, but the widening waves of its tremendous influence are surely making over all later knowledge of human relationships.

In a summary sufficient for our study we may consider the facts as follows:

Reproduction was an efficient process before sex was introduced. For uncounted ages primitive life-forms reproduced by such simple devices as fission, and gemmation—as, indeed, many are still doing. Such reproduction, though wholly adequate for purposes of race-preservation, was not sufficient to carry out the underlying purpose of improvement. Therefore sex was gradually evolved, as a means toward the variation and evolution of species.

Note this carefully in view of much talk about "the life force." Life existed, increased and multiplied in swarming millions, before sex appeared. Sex is more truly to be called "the improvement force."

In very early forms sex is found established in two departments of one body, creating the condition known as hermaphroditism, which, proving useful, was retained, being still common among many plants and some low animal forms. The advantage of sex-distinction being established, it continued to increase until a second organism was developed for sex use only,—a minute, fragile, transient form with but one function,—the first male. Its only power was to contribute its element to the reproductive process carried on by the original organism, later called female; yet its service was so advantageous that the new assistant was retained, and in the course of biologic eras grew to race equality with the female.

As we have so many of life's early sketches still with us, there may be shown, to those unwilling to admit these facts, all manner of primitive males still functioning at a low level of development, such as the tiny male cirrepeds, carried in crevices about her person by the female, and many more common forms, such as the little male spider so soon eaten by his ungrateful mate, or the male bee and ant, of strictly limited usefulness. Indeed, we may still see about us reproduction without fertilization, as with the aphis. This well-known insect, the little green roselouse, can lay eggs that hatch females which continue to lay eggs that hatch females, all summer —fatherless all. But when conditions grow harder, when there is more cold, less food, then she lays eggs which hatch males, and continues to reproduce, with fertilization.

In the field of physical evolution we find three major processes going on, self-preservation, race-preservation, and improvement. There are many forms which have not improved, others which have become decadent, and, from the frequent "missing links," we must infer many to have been eliminated. But in the living world about us the salient facts are along those three general lines: the efforts made by the individual to keep itself alive, the processes by which the race is kept alive, and, most impressive of all, the development of higher forms from lower ones—evolution.

In the varied activities of self-preservation, race characters are developed; in the processes of reproduction we find both race and sex characters; in improvement, the whole stream of differentiating species, new race characters and sex characters are evolved.

With the wide evolution of species, sex has developed along many lines. To the primary differences essential to the initial function have been added many secondary sex-distinctions of varying value. In the male these consist mainly in ornamental appendages, or in the special weapons of sex combat, such as the annual antlers of the stag—an elaborate armament for one brief use.

In the female, however, as the main race type, we find those progressive improvements on which are conditioned all the higher life-forms. From being a mere shedder of helpless germ-cells, as with the oyster, she evolved the more fully developed egg, the marvelous intricacies of the maternal process among insects, viviparous birth, the marsupial pouch, and that highest, most important step in physical reproduction which distinguishes order *mammalia*—lactation.

Beyond perfecting the mechanism for fulfilling his original function, with the decorations and weapons subsidiary to it, the male has contributed nothing more to reproduction save in those instances where he assists the female in the care of the young.

The biological history of sex-evolution is thus briefly sketched in order that we may see the true relative importance of the male and the female throughout nature, and so measure more accurately the effect on human life, notably upon its religious development, of the peculiar preëminence of the male in our species.

Since the very early subjugation of the woman to the man, an unparalleled inversion of all previous sex relationship, we have seen the development of the human race carried on almost exclusively by men, and so inevitably marked by their sex characters. Bearing in mind that she is the race type and he the sex type, we are not surprised to find our progress in social evolution heavily modified to sex; that is, to one sex.

In all the noisy, turbid discussion of the topic which marks our time, we have failed to notice that it is not the two sexes which are so constantly discussed, but only one. This will be clearer if reduced to a simple formula, showing the difference.

We have two sexes; their distinctive processes are these:

FEMALE	MALE
(A) Preliminary union	Preliminary union
(B) Gestation	0
(C) Parturition	0
(D) Lactation	0
(E) Service	Helps in service

In the human race the father, owing to his far higher social development, is the main factor in the service to the child, but it is not that feature of his sex life which he so eagerly discusses. No, his feverish interest, his pathetic overemphasis, is wholly in that primary function, so long his only one, the fertilization of the female. During his period of supremacy he has so lavishly over-indulged this impulse that he has completely lost sight of its purpose, and now, with careful provision for birth-control, he presents to the astonished mother of the world an urgent demand for a relationship wholly divorced from its reason for being, yet which he calls "natural." The fact that an over-sexed female may participate in the desire is no justification. A process more amusingly unnatural could hardly be imagined. Perhaps our nearest approach to it is the custom among the gluttonous old Romans of eating several dinners at once, interspersed with "digestion-control" in the shape of emetics.

In support of his demands and in justification of his desires, man has had at his command all the arts and sciences, the literature, the education, the laws, and, more powerful than all, the religions, of the past. Thus buttressed in self-indulgence, with no dissenting voice except in the complete reaction of asceticism, and with no way of escape for the woman except death, man's misuse of sex has inevitably resulted in its abnormal development in our species.

The extreme competitive instinct of the over-sexed males tended to beat down and eliminate the less sexed; and as only the more highly sexed woman could survive man's ruthless exploitation, she also manifested an excessive development. Had even this been under conditions of frank equality, the results would not have been as bad as they are; but no such equality was accorded.

Following man's early assumption that he alone was the life-giver, and his holding of name and property in the male line, there arose his demand for chastity, first in the wife, later in the girl before marriage. The demand was enforced by most violent penalties, and religion, always on his side, added its supreme commands. So strong and continuous was the pressure that chastity soon became the main virtue required of women, and we have the amazing spectacle of a race of animals in which a tendency was strenuously cultivated in one sex and its indulgence forbidden to the other. It is such paradoxical treatment which has complicated this department of our behavior with perversities and inhibitions. Since the morbid developments of sex in the human race cry to heaven, and since the minds of men do not yet recognize that their attitude is the wrong one, we see now advanced the theory that it is repression which ails us, and that all that is needed to restore us to normality is for women to go as far wrong as men.

Thus completely dominated by sex, in mind as well as in body, man has gone to the length of assuming that his wide superiority in human development is also due to that one power. A conspicuous clergyman of New York clearly states his view that sex and the stomach are the sources of all our achievements. Having reached such a height of inflation in this line that its original expression becomes inadequate, these sex-obsessed theorists hold that their desires must be "sublimated," the "life force" used in other fields of action.

Thus the more normal man, not sex-ridden, who presumes to say, "I am not so incessantly afflicted as you seem to be, but I have accomplished more in service to the world," is met with the assertion, "Yes, but all that you have done is merely another expression of sex!"

They "see red," these people—or shall we call it yellow?—and see nothing else.

To meet their assertions satisfactorily, we must differentiate race characters from sex characters.

The process of evolution, which makes the world about us now so different from what it was in the time when coal was growing, works as before stated, in three main lines, self-preservation, race-preservation, and improvement. Self-preservation has developed many forms and faculties, race-preservation has kept the species alive and strengthened its position, but it is the great underlying push upward which has given us the higher and higher forms of plant and animal life.

It is in such progressive distinction that we find race characters.

All warm-blooded quadrupeds share certain physiological qualities; a cat, a dog, and a hyena have similar respiratory, circulatory, and digestive processes.   The cat, the dog, and the hyena are equally affected by our passionate theorist's "life force," but it does not occupy all their time.

The difference between them—and it is easily perceptible—is due to their race characters.

It is not "sublimated sex" which makes a mouse differ from a rhinoceros, or a pig from a pony. One species is as much moved by sex as another, but it is not due to that impulse that the giraffe's neck grew so long.   There is something going in the world besides the repetition of species, and that is the evolution of better ones.   We may say that there is one underlying force which expresses itself along these three distinct lines, but that is far from picking out a single line of expression and declaring that to be the only one.

In the sum of activities which make up the life of any animal, those of sex are but a small part. Among insects we do find certain stages in a life cycle wholly devoted to the latter, as with butterflies, but even in the case of insects we should hardly attribute the surpassing greediness of the grub, or protective coloration, to "sublimated sex." The only stage where sex may be said to cover all life is among those primitive males which have not yet developed any race qualities at all.

As species advanced, differentiated, grew in size and strength and varied abilities, race qualities came to occupy more and more of the life area; and with genus *Homo*, differing so enormously from all its predecessors, the whole wide range of our special powers, all that makes us "human," is in the line of race qualities.

The superiority of men to women is not a matter of sex at all; it is a matter of race. Social evolution, a force as compelling as any earlier species has known in physical evolution, demands and develops our humanity. Its powers are produced by the exercise of race functions, and these, during human history, have been monopolized by men, forbidden to women.

Men have progressed to our present state of civilization, in all the widening powers of humanity, and have attributed their abilities to their sex; while the painful disabilities which were thus attributable, they called "human nature."

What are the special characteristics of the male, as such? These must be studied not in men alone but in all male creatures, that they may be clearly distinguished from race qualities. So studying them, we find as preëminent and virtually universal: First, the invariably predominant governing passion, everlasting witness of his initial purpose,—desire for the female; secondly, with this, the combative instinct, so useful among competing males; and thirdly, as part of the same main purpose, the instinct of pride and display, so well shown in the peacock.

What are the sex characters of the female, found in all females? These are preponderantly shown in the varied functions of motherhood, to which sex union is but a contributary incident. In the whole wide range of sub-human life we see that her desire for the male is transient, and that the processes of motherhood are her main distinctions.

We are not the only species in which race qualities are monopolized by one sex, but we are the only one in which the monopoly is by the male. The complicated and ceaseless industry of the *Hymenoptera*, the ingenious web and ferocious activities of the *Arachnidæ*, are shown by the female only, so we need not lightly dismiss the charge that the social powers and relationships which make us human are so far exhibited only, or to a preponderant extent, by men.

The race characters of humanity are not far to seek.

Our social development is twofold, partly in the mind, in all the intellectual qualities and high emotions shared by no other creature, and partly in that external manufactured world which we alone produce, and without which we cannot progress.

The family, as an institution, depends on a separate place of residence; trade and commerce, as institutions, depend on means of conveyance, on roads and bridges and ships. In all subhuman life the physical body serves as vehicle and expression of the spirit, but the human spirit, as it rises, expresses itself in and works through material forms we make.

The pride and egotism of the Pharaohs stand pyramidal through the ages; the spiritual fervor of mediæval Europe rises in carven glory to this day (except where the spirit of Germany has turned glory to ruin); periods are known, nations are measured by the things they make.

A nation is a self-supporting group of people who have lived long enough in their own land to have developed a race type and a race culture of their own, with material expression of these in the things they make. Gipsies, who merely travel about, living in other people's countries and producing nothing, are a people, perhaps, but not a nation.

People by millions, of one racial stock, may live for ages in one land without becoming a nation, as is seen among the tribes of Africa. Even the magnificent civic development of ancient Greece fell short of national development; the Greeks were citizens but not nationals.

All the heights of human achievement are attained by the exercise of race qualities, and follow the lines of an ever-widening and intensifying power of spirit, expressed in nobler and more efficient material forms. It is this development in the human spirit and in human work which has been denied to women, and which men have innocently supposed to be masculine because they attained it. Every form of effort outside the home was called "man's work," and so variously given pay and honor, while what was still done in the home was called "woman's work," and given neither.

It is amusing to see how rapidly the attitude toward a given occupation changed as it changed hands. For instance, two of the oldest occupations of women, the world over, were that of helping other women to bring babies into the world and that of laying out the dead. Women sat at the gates of life, at both ends, for countless generations. Yet so soon as the obstetrician found one large source of income in his highly specialized services, and the undertaker found another in his, these occupations became "man's work"; a "woman doctor" was shrunk from even by women, and a "woman undertaker" seemed ridiculous.

In neither case is any sex quality involved.   It
was of course more natural for women to help one
another in childbirth than for a man to take part
in that performance (the obstetrician has but one
companion in nature, the "obstetric frog"), but
whether performed by man or by woman this
service and that of preparing the dead for burial
are distinctions of humanity, not of sex.

There is no more salient human characteristic
than language.   It is the essential vehicle of
transmitted thought, and in its fixed form, as literature, makes that thought a continuing supply.
Our libraries are miraculous permanent forms of
what without them would have died with individual bodies, or trickled crookedly from mind to
mind by "word of mouth."

That this invaluable human characteristic first
developed through peacefully working groups of
women does not make it feminine, and the reten-
tion of all its higher uses by men for so long does
not make it masculine.

Also the origins of that noble height of human
achievement we call art are found in the work
of women.   The decorative instinct is human, not
sexual, and as woman was the first to make

things, so she was the first to decorate them.
Later, as man made anything,—a canoe, a
weapon,—he felt the same human impulse, and
decorated it.

Music, in its beginnings, seems more masculine. It is the male who make the love-noises
and war-noises, in lower species; the wooer turns
as naturally to the serenade as the mother to the
lullaby; triumph also expresses itself in extra
sounds: the hen cackles cheerfully when she has
laid an egg, and the cock crows cheerfully when
he has n't. But music in its higher stages has far
outgrown its sex basis and become a human art.

In all the development of art, however, we find
its natural progress as a race characteristic griev-
ously interfered with by its monopoly as "man's
work." His natural proclivities are marked
enough, but his excessive development in sex has
made his influence in human work too conspicuous to be denied; and nowhere is it more plainly
shown than in works of art.

Here we have a form of expression, appearing
naturally as a sort of flowering of what Veblen
calls "The instinct of workmanship," giving
pleasure to the maker and to the beholder. The

lovely impulse, growing with our growth, has developed all manner of vehicles, of mediums, of methods. The simple industries and as simple decorations of primitive women have reached such heights as are shown in rugs and shawls of the Orient, the embroideries of China and Japan, the rich tapestries of old Europe.

Two forces have marred this glory of humanity, one the "commercialization" which results from a masculized industry, and the other a corrupting spirit of egotism which blasphemes against an ultra-human function by making it mere "self-expression."

Self-expression is an essentially masculine attribute. Man's primal function involves exactly that. His very splendors of gay color and floating plumage, of crest and comb and mane and whiskers, are due to what Ward calls "male effloresence," or what present-day theorists would dub "sublimated sex."

Art furnished a new medium for this output. As man, through long indulgence, has grown more and more over-sexed, and has found in his own proper person no way to show it,—even his normal distinction of Jovian locks and beard be-

ing disallowed,—the accumulating surplus has
burgeoned forth as best it might, in human expression. In art it cries aloud. His personality, his name, his vital need of putting himself
into his work, has reached such ludicrous heights
that a picture, a statue, is described not as such
but as a given surname—"a Jones" or "a Smith."

The man wishes to "live" through his work;
he thirsts for fame; it is his name, his personality
which must be remembered. Again, and carefully, let it be stated that here is no reflection on
the original value of the masculine tendency.
The objection is first to its over-development, and
secondly to its injurious effect on the normal
growth of humanity. Every human function is
developed for human service, and art is one of the
greatest. It should illuminate and rejoice the
world, adding pleasure in production, and delight
in appreciation, to millions upon millions.

As it is, we find the world going hungry for
beauty, while the artist sits up nights to find out
exactly how he feels, and paint a picture to "tell
the world." The world does not particularly
care; why should it? One of the first things we

teach our children is to check a too-boisterous self-expression; the breeding of a gentleman involves a decent self-restraint.

No artist, man or woman, can help legitimate self-expression: that inheres in personality. We do not talk alike, write alike, or paint alike. Even when trained in some "school" or "period" of art, one artist differeth from another in magnitude. The error lies in a too-concentrated attention upon personality, a sort of inflammation of the ego.

Suppose three artists sat down to paint a golden marsh at sunset; one having a headache, one a heartache, and one a toothache. The picture should at least seek to represent the marsh and not the malady.

The most general field of human functioning is economic.

Here we stand alone in minute specialization, in complex organization, in all the subtle and varied skill and profound efficiency with which we serve our common needs. Work is human. It is not feminine, though women began it. It is not masculine, though men have taken it. But because men have kept women out of it for so long, it has shared in the disadvantages of excessive masculinity.

As a race quality, work means social service. Every variety of human work is developed for the advantage of others. No solitary human being exists to compare with, but those who live in the smallest groups do the least work; and vice versa.

As a race quality this social function should manifest a widening pleasure and a rising power, with an increase in efficiency in trade, in commerce, in business, which ought long since to have spread to the ends of the earth our best advantages. But work, under a sex monopoly, has been so overwhelmingly marked by masculine characteristics that the business of the world is frankly regarded by men as a field of warfare, a process in which to get ahead of one another, by which to seize for one's self what another has made.

CHAPTER V

THE POWER AND THE PURPOSE OF WOMEN

NOT all the long, loud struggle for "women's rights," not the varied voices of the "feminist movement," not the growing claims for "sex equality," and, most particularly, not the behavior of "emancipated women," have given us any clear idea of the power and purpose of the mother sex.

The race mind, obsessed for thousands of years with world-wide convictions as to the inferior and subsidiary nature of the female, is not able in one generation to change its attitude. Even where the newly known biological facts are understood, there is no immediate and thorough change in the deep-rooted, widely ramified sex-complex which underlies and is so interwoven with our whole system of thought.

One may show incontrovertibly that a small green snake is harmless, but the hearer's attitude toward the reptile does not necessarily change. One may show that the common house-fly is far more dangerous than a snake, but no shuddering repulsion is aroused.

A new concept must be very heartily accepted, and forced into connection with conduct, either by a habit of bringing one's hehavior into line with a logical perception, or, as is more common, by some strong emotion.   The habit of acting up to one's belief is rarely found, and as to emotion, one of the strongest emotions known to us is that which still regards women from the "cave man" point of view.

Some space must be given, therefore, to presentation of the real status of the female in life, and of her relation to the development of the race.

First fix the mind on the fact that reproduction can go on without fertilization, that many early forms of life have endured till now without sex; that from such early forms there was developed, not an Eve from a spare rib, but a tiny and temporary assistant, the male, while the original organism, later called female, continued its race activities.

Holding this fact securely, place it beside that popular concept of woman as "God's last best gift to man," and see what happens. If the mind is free and logical, a total change in our mental attitude must follow, so great and far-reaching as to stand second only to that which results from the acceptance of evolution as life's main process. And if it is not? Why, then we exert that morbid mental power forcibly developed in us by ages of unassimilable beliefs; we isolate this new precept as if it were a theorem in higher mathematics, and go on feeling and acting as if it were not there.

Let us follow it to its logical conclusion, heartily assisted by more facts along the way. We find in all early forms the brief and precarious life of the male useful only in his initial purpose, the fertilization of the female. We find him slowly developing into equality with her, and acquiring certain distinctions used in sex combat or sex attraction which have been fondly thought to make him her superior. But the stag is no better deer for all his antlers, the peacock no better fowl for all his tail.

Whatever constitutes the distinctive qualities of the species is found fully developed in the female; she is the race type.

In any careful study of the human species, we must recognize the same fact: woman is the race type of humanity.

Yet the world we see shows small proof of it. It is a man's world, for good or bad. Any super-mundane naturalist, applying his microscope to our human activities, would find the male every-where in evidence, carrying on all the distinctive human activities, while the female is segregated to the functions of sex, combined with those of domestic service.

His position, relative to other men and to so-ciety, has varied and improved from century to century, the hunter changing to the breeder of cat-tle, to the farmer, and so, through every line of trade and craft, profession and science, up to the complicated thing we call civilization; while her position, relative to him alone, has changed mainly in the external forms of that relation. The feminist movement of which recent decades have been so full, is but of the moment; back of it, still going on beneath it, and all around and

behind it, lies the unbroken influence of ages of
over-sexed subjugation.

The civilization so produced, so heavily dominated by the sex less fitted to represent humanity,
is so admittedly defective that many hold we have
made no real progress at all.   This is not true,
but it is true that our progress has been cruelly
hindered and perverted, making human life a
shame and a misery when it might long since have
become a pride and a joy.

We must learn to study normal human life as
the outcome of the feminine nature, and to see
that many features we have assumed to be natural
to humanity are merely natural to masculinity,
which is quite another thing.

With the opposite point of view we are quite
familiar: men assuming themselves to be the
normal human beings, deprecating the influence
of women as "feminine," objecting strongly to a
dreaded "feminization."

The term "masculization," which is precisely
as regular in form and which describes a far more
common fact, we do not yet recognize.

If it were possible to lay aside for the moment
our long-held misconceptions, and look at human

life as much more legitimately developed through the female, what kind of world should we see?

Normal sex, in the female, is a means to motherhood. The female's attraction for and use of the male is solely as a preliminary to motherhood. The higher, longer companionship due to monogamy was brought about by its advantage to the offspring. The father, as an active assistant in the care of the young, shares in the duties of motherhood, and is developed by them, as she has been. But a natural monogamy does not imply continuous sex use.

Race activities, developed by changing conditions, the female has always manifested as fully as the male. Up through all the stages below us the female shares with the male in every formative influence, transmits her improvement to her young, and adds to it by the enlarging benefits of maternal care.

If such a condition remains, in humanity, we should see the female progressing through every opening line of human work, learning all that was to be known, practising all that was to be done, keeping step with the male in all his social growth.

All this has been prevented, ostensibly in the name of motherhood.   Motherhood, we have been told, prevents women from fulfilling other activities.   Its holiness, its sanctity, its indispensability have been stoutly maintained by the sex-biased, illogical minds which could approve such use of a wife as to impair her motherhood, and which found no difficulty in combining her "sacred" functions with those of a cook and chambermaid.

If motherhood were really free and normal in humanity, its influence would be along these lines:

Being human, conscious, intelligent, that which has been so long a merely instinctive process would become telic, guided by knowledge and will.   Lower mothers have improved their species without knowledge or thought.   The highest kind of mother, bringing the best thought and knowledge of the world to bear on her great work, would face it with reverence and with a noble pride.

Is the race weak?   She can make it strong. Is it stupid?   She can make it intelligent.   Is it foul with disease?   She can make it clean.

Whatever qualities she finds desirable she can develop in the race, through her initial function as a mother—selection. This is her duty as a sex function, and her duty as a member of a great race. We should have conventions of young women gathered to study what is most needed in their race and how they may soonest develop it. For instance, far-seeing Japanese women might determine to raise the standard of height, or patriotic French women determine to raise the standard of fertility, or wise American women unite with the slogan, "No more morons!"

Such an attitude is sound in biology and in civics; yet it strikes us coldly, seems strange, almost revolting. In all our man-ridden past the mother has been so subordinate to the father that we cannot dissociate her immense power as a race-builder from a mere personal sentiment. The very word "free" in connection with motherhood suggests merely a loose relationship; though it visibly means freedom of choice of one father, not several.

A decisive word here as to monogamy:

"Man," said good Mr. Howells, "is as yet an imperfectly monogamous animal." All along

the years behind us we have had the laughable
spectacle of a species endeavoring to maintain
two kinds of sex relationship at once, the woman
monogamous, the man promiscuous. To-day
we see on the one hand an effort to establish a
"single standard" upward, demanding of men the
same chastity they have demanded of women;
and on the other, a sickening decline of the
mother sex to the debased habits of the male.

By the present-day school of promiscous relations any talk of monogamy is branded as "Vic-
torian," "Puritanical," "bourgeois," or in worse
terms if possible. These ignorant people do not
seem to know that monogamy is just as "natural"
among higher species of mammals and birds as
promiscuity is among insects and reptiles.

Nature is no prude. She knows not Victoria
from Messalina, nor bourgeois from birth-con-
troller. She allows every form of sex union
which produces the best results in a given species, and discourages by a death sentence those
which do not.

It is not civil law nor social law nor moral law
that develops monogamy; it is biological law,
which no informed mind repudiates, which can

never be broken with impunity. When it is to the advantage of the young to have the continued care of two parents, then monogamy appears. With it are developed the subtle and tender ties which have reached the high beauty known as romantic love, in us and also, to a degree, in those below us living under the same law. You may kill one of a pair of mated leopards and the other will follow you to the death; and with some birds, if one of a pair dies, the other will not mate again.

A free and conscious motherhood in humanity would have long ago realized the value of monogamy, and have enforced it. How? By the simple process of not mating with any other kind of male, not mating in any other kind of way. Is it not easy?—no legal enactments, no punishment; merely a wise, free womanhood, with standards of right and wrong based on natural law, and putting those standards into practice.

Such motherhood, fully educated and realizing the value of education to the child, would long since have seen to it that no child grew up without the best education possible. Compare the natural growth of free human motherhood with the enforced ignorance of a slave-motherhood and the admired ignorance of a pet-motherhood, with their effects on the race.

Merely as mothers, and without reference to the higher powers of humanity, women would have tended to produce a better world had they held their natural place, but far beyond that is the growth of a normal humanity, which has been so retarded by the exclusion of its "better half."

Not until we attained the idea of evolution as the main law of life did any of us dream that we were a growing race instead of a stationary or a fallen one. The whole world lay under the burden of a gloomy misconception, a wholesale inferiority-complex which paralyzed effort, denied hope, and made ambition a thing for the scorn of philosophers.

With new knowledge of geologic time, which shows us to be a young species even physically, while our social growth has but started, we can face our problems with courage and hope and forgive our early sins as one forgives the blunders of a baby. Here is no world of helpless, groveling little creatures, "born unto trouble, as the sparks fly upward," and soon to be snatched out of a brief and miserable trial here to an endless misery or bliss hereafter, equally undeserved. No, our race is the highest work of God, developed so far by the forces of natural law, with its further development in its own hands. There is no need to worry about the shortcomings of our ancestors, immediate or remote; our business is to determine where we are going and how best to get there. But here the average mind instantly harks back to the old version, so pitifully individual: "What shall I do to be saved?"

Our question is a race question quite beyond any individual concern. No one in one brief lifetime can produce perfection, but the race can work toward perfection and approach more closely to it in every generation.

The builders and decorators of the great cathedrals of the past gave successive lifetimes to the gradual perfection of a mighty work. Can we not hold the same attitude toward the mightiest work of God, the human race?

The human mother, by virtue of her preponderant share in the high process of race-building, comes naturally to this point of view. The sub-human mother accomplished her task by instinct, without thought, and caring only for her own. Women, because of their arrested development through unnatural subjection to the male, have been held down to that sub-human level, prompted only by instinct and caring only for their own. By such limitation they fail not only in the very service to their own they strive for but in their large duty to the race.

What we may hope for from a general realization by women of this race duty, is a tremendous surge upward of all our race standards. Here is no abstract science requiring years of study to understand, and slow painful efforts to put in practice. For women already educated enough to grasp the facts and their relations, and able to make a conviction work, it should require no more than a book or two, a lecture or two, to start swifter social evolution. Such women, organized for the greatest work ever undertaken,— the awakening of human motherhood,—could educate every growing girl in the new sense of hope, purpose, and power. They would be like a vast new army sweeping in to help exhausted forces, broken and discouraged.   In some thirty years these aroused women could send forth a new kind of people to help the world; better born; better trained; able to discriminate and reason, to judge wisely, and strong to carry out their decisions.

All this was opened to us by the perception of evolution, the law of growth.   And what have we made of it?   As religion has been modified by the mind of man, so has science.   Man is by nature inherently combative, and all he has gathered from the great law that governs the unfolding of a bud, the sprouting of a seed, the hatching of an egg, is that shop-worn shibboleth, "The struggle for existence, and the survival of the fittest."

The very language is heavily masculized.   Because by nature the competitive male makes of his efforts either a race or a fight, because his strongest impulse next to desire for the female is to outdo and overcome another male, he describes every kind of effort as "fighting."   The dying man "fights" for his breath; the kind nurse, the wise physician are "fighting with death"; even the Christian, follower of the Prince of Peace, is said to be "fighting the good fight," encouraged by "Onward, Christian soldiers, marching as to war."

This is all foolish, merely another proof of our masculized condition. Evolution is not one universal row; it is growth, and can be greatly assisted by cultivation. Mr. Burbank's garden is not an arena. Breeders of cattle do not seek to improve the stock by setting the sires to fight one another.

Farms are not cultivated, ships are not sailed, houses are not built, books are not written by fighting. One would think that agriculture alone would long since have taught us that the way to improve any living thing is to take care of it. Do we cast our seed in among whatever else is growing and leave it to take its chance? Do we allow every weed to flourish, that our corn may compete with it and the fittest survive? No; we want corn, and we do everything we know how to prepare the soil, add special food and water, and remove the competitors—"fighting the weeds," we call it. See the six-foot man with the hoe *fighting* a bit of "pusley"!

Growth is the major process of nature, and

cultivation is the greatest help to growth, which, carried to a perfectly obvious conclusion, shows us a growing human race, and points to the need of cultivation, to help it grow.

Instead of which we see a world where the major activity, the one most honored and honorably recorded, is fighting. Those who fed and clothed and housed the world, those who taught it, those whose far-reaching minds looked ahead and pointed out improvements, with all the inventors whose contributions have done more than anything else to promote our advance in spite of our best efforts not to move—they were not made into little lead dolls for boys to play with, nor their statues set up in every town.

If our women were fully human, if they had caught up with man in race-development and their influence were as strong in world-management as his has been, we should have a very different standard of values.

Every human act and quality is to be measured by its effect on the race. If it' does not affect the race in one way or another, it is of no consequence. If it is disadvantageous, it is wrong; if advantageous, it is right. And those who do most to help the advance of humanity are to be most honored.

Where women have failed and still fail in their race duty, is in their over-modification to sex, their continued submission to traditions and conventions forced upon them in the past, and, at present, their frequent contemptible surrender to previously masculine vices and weaknesses. No prisoned harem beauty, no victim of white-slavery, no dull-eyed kitchen drudge is so pitiful as these "new women," free, educated, independent, and just as much the slaves of fashion and the victims of license as they were before.

It is of course inevitable that centuries of subjugation should weaken the spirit and dull the mind; and that the currents of associated sex habit should still run strong where no independent brain action is set up against them.

The marvel is that in spite of this there are so many women pressing on, surmounting all disadvantages, and making their influence felt already in sterling work for world-improvement.

With every year there will be more of them, and their children, differently reared, will be a new force in the world. Never has so large and swift a change come upon the world, and never one of such fundamental value. The mother sex, the main line of humanity, is coming into action, and all the trouble and distress, the shame and foul disease, the unhappiness and confusion ensuant upon her checked development will so in time be outgrown.

THE PRIMAL POWER

Would ye plant the earth with new-made men?
   A race new-born, a race unstained?
Clothed in flesh that hath no flaw,
One with nature, one with law,
   Strong-souled, clear-brained?

This may motherhood achieve,
   Full-grown mothers brave and free,
Splendid bodies trained and strong,
Hearts that ache for human wrong,
   Eyes that can see.

Learning new their primal power,
   A reign forgot, a crown disowned;
Rising from their prison blind,
Pets and servants of mankind,
   Re-born, re-throned.

Theirs the power beyond appeal
   To choose the good, reject the base;
So shall all degenerate blood
Die, forbidden fatherhood—
   So rise our race!

CHAPTER VI

BEHAVIOR, CONSCIOUS AND UNCONSCIOUS

THERE are those, Walter Pater amongst them, who speak reverently of the superiority of "being" over "doing." Many who read or hear, but do not think, have been impressed by this suggestion, and sagaciously repeat that it is nobler To Be than To Do.

To such let us put this simple query: Can you mention any form of life that can "be" without doing anything? A stone can "be" for a long time, but we should hardly call it nobler than a growing plant or a moving animal.

Life is action. We should not say "life" as a noun but "living" as an active verb. The process of living is a continuously active one; it depends on the incessant performance of some functions and the frequent or occasional performance of others.

Our internal unconscious activity is needed to

maintain physical life, and all social life and progress depend upon our external activity, both genetic and telic, both through our unconscious reactions and our determined conduct.

The lightest study of physical evolution shows us that "function comes before organ," that muscles are developed by use.

Suppose a bird should assert that "being" was better than flying, and sit still. He would not "be" very long.

But, urges the approver of "being," surely a man can be wise, be good, be great! Is not so desirable a state nobler than the efforts to attain to it?

If a man never did anything, we should not know whether he was wise or unwise, good or bad, great or small. If he does wise good and great acts, we judge him by them, and by them only.

He can, of course, make a reputation, and then sit down on it, not doing anything more, but such behavior is distinctly not noble. Character is formed, and maintained, only by action.

The form and special distinction of any living thing is the balanced total of its activities.

I 'm not feathers, beak, and wings,
A bird that flies, a bird that sings,—
　No, you have the handle wrong;
　By what gifts to me belong
　I am Flying, I am Song.

With the human race we find a far more complicated field of conduct than with simpler organisms.　Even without our power of conscious direction we should feel the often contradictory pressure of the social and the personal heredity.

The direct force of personal heredity we share with all other animals, we react to the influence of the environment as do other animals, but we have a supreme distinction all our own, the power of governing conduct by ideas.　Such an abstraction as duty, for instance, holding the captain to his ship till it sinks under him, is not to be paralleled even by the devotion of a dog to orders.

Under the influence of an idea, a theory, a belief, right or wrong, rational or absurd, human beings are able to modify their conduct in direct opposition to any or all other forces.

One crucial illustration may be given which

ought to convince any rational being of the power of an idea over our actions.

You are supposed to be traveling, observing human behavior, and have reached the Marquesas Islands, where you chance upon this scene: a man lies face downward upon the earth; another man, squatting by his side, is busily engaged in hammering a sharp shell into and along the skin of the prostrate one. The sufferer is not tied down. He makes no complaint. He just lies there and lets the other man make long, intricate furrows in his epidermis.

Just imagine for a moment any other living creature voluntarily submitting to a prolonged anguish like this!

But man is a reasoning being; doubtless this man has some good reason for the endurance test. Not at all. There is no real advantage resultant from it. What power, then, holds him down, makes him suppress his groans and submit to hours of torture?

The power of an idea—that is all. And a foolish idea at that. The poor vain thing imagines that he is more beautiful when copiously tattooed! Sometimes the whole body of one of these islanders is covered with intricate lace-like patterns, of which the exhibiter is as proud as is any duchess of her rose-point.

There are plenty of other instances of physical pain and mutilation endured under the pressure of false ideas, but none more satisfying than this. Among boys, and an ignorant class of men such as common sailors, the primitive custom of tattooing still exerts its old-time sway, guilelessly proving the power of "mind over matter" even when the mind is ridiculously wrong.

Physical pain is nothing to us, natural laws are nothing to us, heredity and environment alike are set aside, under the supreme dominance of an accepted idea.

A very pretty instance of such dominance is seen in that story of Kipling's in which a remotely placed Englishman, living in a wild forest with only a native servant, "dressed for dinner" each night. This apparently incomprehensible action he performed, it was stated, to preserve his self-respect.

Clothing has always been largely a matter of symbolism. The Ethiopian may not be able to change his skin, but he can certainly change his appearance outside of it. In uniform, livery, habit, and robe we express ideas, and those ideas react upon us and upon our conduct.

That unconscious conduct which would lead us naturally to put on warm clothes in winter and cool ones in summer, is an imperceptible influence compared with the conscious conduct based on many considerations other than temperature. I have seen women, both young women and old, standing on a street corner in zero weather, in a searching wind, with a wide bare space over the bronchial region and the apices of the lungs, and wearing thin skirts reaching but little below the knees, diaphanous silk stockings, and slippers. Yet if those women had been seized upon and muffled to the ears and ankles in warm woolen, with woolen hose and "arctics" on their feet, they would have been extremely uncomfortable.

One would think that physical discomfort, even pain, would be harder to bear than the pressure of a wholly arbitrary and foolish concept, but it is not. Humanity is far more strongly affected by what is in its mind than by all the world outside. Such primal instincts as those of eating, of mating, of self-preservation are of no avail against some religious theory which requires fasting, celibacy, or full martyrdom.

It is the variety of governing forces, their intermixture and interplay, which make the study of human conduct so peculiarly complicated.

Take, for instance, that human performance called a wedding, and untangle the various forces which produce it. There is the primary reproductive force; the added force of sex attraction; to the woman, the potent influence of economic advantage; to the man, the possession of a private cook. Then come the blended lines of social heredity, determining many details of law and custom, with race-mixture, class-distinction, degree of education all contributing. Then the powerful pressure of religion, the professional side of which long since seized upon birth, death, and marriage as invaluable bases of dominance.

Compare this intricacy with the essential simplicity of mating among other creatures, and we have a good instance of the difficulties confronting the student of human conduct.

These difficulties are by no means insuperable, however. The main lines of influence are easily disentangled, their causes and results shown.

In this study the main issue is an indication of the influence of masculinity upon religion, a thing fully exhibited through all history; and with it a projection of the influence of femininity when that force really expresses itself. The latter must be more deductive and inferential than the former, on account of the peculiar subordination of women during our entire history, yet it is clearly distinguishable in both its primitive tendencies and its unsuppressible persistence.

In the field of unconscious conduct we may watch mankind vary, develop, and fall back, like any other species, according to changes in soil, climate, food supply, enemies, and other natural conditions.

But in that of conscious conduct we see him change his soil by drainage, irrigation, and fertilization; defy climate by fire, clothing, and artificial cooling; develop his food supply out of all comparison with that of any other creature; and in regard to enemies he has overcome so many that his race succeeds in living virtually everywhere on earth. As to his own habits, consciously directed, many of them are impossible to account for, save as the result of ideas—true, false and foolish.

Seeing is not merely an effect of light on the retina but what the brain gathers from that image. Our conduct is not directly governed by facts and laws of nature but by our knowledge of, or theories about them. There is no real connection between meeting a black cat and going on a journey, but this irrelevant animal has stopped many.

When we study the evils which still make human life a byword for misery, we find most of them to be of man's own making. The Eskimo is happy in an arctic climate, the South Sea Islander in a tropical one. But civilized man can be unhappy in any climate, through his own misdeeds.

This has been plain to thinking persons from the first. The puzzle before all philosophers was how to account for the behavior of mankind, and their guesses at an answer vary widely. Other creatures do what is good for them, without instruction; man continually does what is not good for him, in spite of the best advice.

Thinking is a pleasure, a normal organic function. Asking questions shows the appetite of a healthy brain. The less one knows, the more freely he can imagine and the more questions he can ask, as in the case of a child.

So we see the early thinker using his brain with passionate eagerness, devising theories of superb range and daring, coming to towering conclusions of terrible importance, and promulgating them with none to contradict—except, indeed, those in other lands who had erected other theories.

When that unfurnished brain began to see logical connection between its childlike assumptions, when a percept was made, the primitive thinker really felt that he had heard a voice. His idea he promulgated with the solemn prefix, "And God said unto me,"—whatever god he worshiped. As priesthood became a profession,—became, indeed, the most powerful and profitable profession in the world,—that quite natural persuasion grew into accepted inspiration, and the conscious use of revelation became the strongest engine in maintaining mastery.

The sanctity of the priesthood, in ages of constant warfare, gave them a chance to grow old, gave them time to think and to teach what they knew, to their close corporation. Through their picked and protected brains came most of our early progress in science and art. But other classes were not encouraged to think; they must obey. The soldiers with their dangerous power, the peasantry with their indispensable services must be subordinate, and are yet.

For any social progress it was imperative that the conduct of man should be regulated. His hit-or-miss behavior, unreliable and often injurious, must be brought into line with the common advantage. Yet it was not contemplated that he should become intelligent and self-controlled. In those simple early days compulsion was the only known method of changing conduct, so priest and king made laws and regulations and strove to enforce them.

The priest was not a fighting-man. The soldier had the advantage in physical force, even before an organized state took command of the enforcement of law. The hold of the priesthood must be over the mind, and so has been from the first.

This is not a charge of long-planned, definite purpose. It is simply an explanation of how every current of self-interest and class interest would combine with the most solid convictions of serving the people, to develop the machinery of superstitious terror by which alleged consequences in another world were used to compel submission in this.

We may grope among the conditions of very early savagery to find the bases of our feelings of sanctity, mystery, and terror associated with religion. Terror we have seen accounted for by the ghost-haunted nightmares following upon unbridled feasting. As soon as it became obligatory to give to the priests part of the profits of the hunt, the firstlings of the flock, or the cream of the crops, they were able to eat more frequently and fully than other people, and doubtless had more dreams—a vicious circle.

Underworked and overfed, using their brains and not their bodies, it is easy to see how their visions grew upon them. The sense of terror once established, it was the best handle of power and so maintained.

To preserve the terror, there must be no familiar inquiry into who ate the sacrifices, or any other details of the sheltered life. "The sanctuary" was necessary, and was soon set up and guarded by every known art.

The notion of mystery, so needless to the sunlit truths of rational religion, probably had its origin in the ancient sex taboos. Here began separation and concealment, things hidden and forbidden, with punishment for any who dared look. The peculiar and sometimes dreadful rites of initiation for boy and girl at the age of puberty, the special marks of distinction adopted by one sex and forbidden the other,—a prejudice still strong among us,—all these customs developed in the human mind that remarkable product, a muffled thought process.

A mystery is not merely a thing you do not know; it is a thing you must not know, which it is wrong to think about.

An odd idea, this! But child or savage takes easily to it; it soon became a race habit of mind, and the priesthood seized upon it as a wonderful protection for their imperfect thought.

Some religious theory or doctrine would be developed which was absurd enough to rouse comment and question. That would never do. So there grew up, as naturally as a running vine, the wonderfully interlocking self-protective structure of a great religion,—any of the religions; they are all alike in this claim,—"Here is something more important than anything else: it must be believed; if you do not believe you will be terribly punished."

Since it was apparent that believers in other religions were tolerably prosperous, the punishment was alleged to take place after death— when none could contradict.

One wonders here whether our hideous hell-idea was developed to meet the persecutions of early Christianity. Since the torments inflicted upon people in this life were terrible beyond belief, it was necessary to think up something sufficiently worse to strengthen the martyr to endurance. And—wonderful tribute to the power of a concept!—the fear of a hypothetical roasting in hell enabled men to endure very practical roasting in this.

By the power of ideas over conduct each religion maintains its hold; and since the hold is absolutely dependent upon the ideas, it becomes a sin to doubt them. The more patently absurd they may be, the more necessary it is that they be shrouded by mystery, guarded by sanctity.

The enormous influence of religion upon conduct is obvious. Unfortunately, the conduct demanded was seldom of any value in promoting our happiness and progress, but mostly concerned those rites and ceremonies and those sacrifices either in goods or money essential to the maintenance of the established religion.

One of the first and worst of the evil effects of religion on conduct was through the theory of fatalism. This doctrine, so abhorrent to all common sense, has fascinated the mind of millions. At bottom it is the simple "I can't help it," of failure. But at top it becomes a towering theory of Fate, of Kismet, of Predestination. In common usage, we find it in the gambler's belief in luck, in our solemn term "Destiny," in the Scotch acceptance, "A man maun dree his weird."

Against it in the civilized world stand all the things that we have achieved. Under its paralyzing weight lie the stationary racial cultures, the people trained for ages in submission. The casuist explains that what we do accomplish is not to our credit; that, too, is Fate. Which reminds me of a story:

There was once a class in ethics, with an earnest teacher trying to show the value of this conduct rather than that. One of those attending was a fatalist, and his remarks tended to prove it quite useless for anybody to do anything.

"Do I understand you correctly?" asked the teacher. "Is your position this: That a good man is not to be praised for his actions, which are due to his heredity and environment; that he is not good from his own will but because he cannot help it; and similarly that we should not blame the bad man for his misdeeds; he too is only bad because he cannot help it?"

The fatalist acknowledged that that was precisely what he meant.

Then said the teacher to the class: "Hereafter, when our brother rises to talk to us about fatalism, you must not blame him for talking to harm us, nor praise him for talking to help us; he is only talking because he can't help it."

After which his words had no effect other than to rouse laughter.

Where so much depended on training the mind of man to understand, to know, and above all to act on knowledge, religion taught him to believe, and to obey, with his ghastly background of helplessness. Even in Christianity, as developed through the churches, we have that effect of helplessness, and are taught that everything has to be done for us, that our best attitude is as

A broken and empty vessel
Fit for the Master's use.

Christianity also has implanted in our minds the concept of our essential unworthiness, a most injurious doctrine. Every wise teacher of children knows how paralyzing it is for the child to become convinced that he is naughty. Yet the child world has been taught that for centuries. With religion as unquestionably our strongest help in concept-governed conduct it is especially pitiable that so many of its major concepts have been wrong.

Women, too, had our doctrines come through them, would doubtless have shown various errors in religious concepts, but these would have been of a different nature. It is quite possible that the female might have discriminated against the male had she had sole power. But with her as his companion, modifying but not obliterating his influence, a better balance would have been preserved. We should have avoided that general prejudice born of the exclusive rule of man, which called all the conduct natural to him "human nature" and all that was natural to her "feminine." His conduct he assumed to be typical of the race, and hers he deprecated as weak and unworthy.

This position has affected our behavior both in its unconscious and its conscious expression. Our very word "virtue" comes from *vir*, a man. To bear pain or face disaster "like a man" is a compliment, but "to grouse like a woman," as Kipling terms her complaining, is anything but a compliment. Yet when we study the man's and the woman's relative capacity for courage and endurance, we find small basis for invidious distinction.   Ask the dentist!

The underlying facts are these: The tendency to combat, which involves men, from boyhood up, in real or playful fighting, and in games which are really battles, necessarily involves their hurting one another; but the merciless ridicule which is bestowed on the sufferer if he complains, makes him bear it in silence.   Moreover, in the joy of combat, the excitement and passionate violence of exertion, hurts are not noticed.   A man may skin his knuckles in knocking down his adversary and not even notice it, but when he hits his thumb with a hammer, while doing useful work, he is not so oblivious.

Women, on the other hand, have no impulse to bang one another about.   An injury from violence gives them neither pride nor pleasure.   Also, it may injure their attractiveness, which is a business asset.   A broken nose or a "cauliflower ear" does not disqualify a man for marriage; either is a disadvantage to a woman.

But when it comes to meeting disappointment and disaster, or to bearing pain from disease, women show certainly as much courage as men. A man who is "ruined" is sometimes quite unable to bear it, so he shoots himself and leaves his wife and children to bear it without him. In his own special and most intense desire he is notably unable to stand interference and denial, but shoots his rival, shoots the girl, and shoots himself, indiscriminately. The effect of the highest religious ideas upon this field of masculine conduct has always been negligible.

The conduct of women was virtually all within the range of domestic life. Their existence was always that of a female relative, daughter, sister, sweetheart, wife, mother, grandmother, aunt, and so on. They had small relation with any men outside their own circle, or with other women. It is but a limited portion of the conduct of women which can be measured as "human," and even that is influenced by their sex, as man's conduct is by his.

The motherliness of women makes them invaluable servants, in business as in the home. That impulse to give, to serve, and to keep at it indefinitely, is very good for the employer, but very bad for the woman. In her early years of outside work she is limited in usefulness by her constant lookout for the more permanent job of matrimony; but if she stays at work, unmarried, she is faithful and endlessly serviceable.

In the field of unconscious conduct the natural tendencies of women are more humanly useful than those of men. In conscious conduct women are influenced by ideas as man is; but the governing ideas of the world, notably in religion, are mainly his.

When the unwritten laws of womanhood are as potent as those we hear so much of among men, and when the written ones also are partly made by woman, we may look for widely interesting changes in conduct.

CHAPTER VII

MORALS AND CONDUCT

THE strange and contradictory course of human conduct, pulled and driven here and there by various forces, is heavily influenced by what we call morals. Morals are simply *mores*, tribal customs. By long use and inheritance they settle into race habits, almost instincts, and are thought "right" merely because of long usage.

The changing conditions of life demand a change in moral valuation, which is always resisted by a past-worshiping people. A recent and familiar instance is the passing of that essentially masculine and long-established custom of the duel. Prompt resentment of any slight to his "honor" was expected of every gentleman, and he who was slighted challenged the slighter to fight with him. If he killed the offender, then his offended "honor" was avenged. If the offender killed the offended, which often happened, at any rate the latter died "on the field of honor"—which must have been a great comfort to his widow.

Very slowly, under the pressure of new ideas, —probably the strengthening of the mind brought about by widening education,—this approved feature in the conduct of a gentleman was outgrown. It still lingers even now among backward people, as, for instance, German students, who maintain the primitive custom in full force, and are as proud of their foolish scars as any Marquesan of his tattooing.

Young people are prone to maintain ancient customs long after those older and wiser have given them up. Clear proof of this is shown in the persistence of the remote and hideous savage custom of initiation by torture, which is still followed by school and college-boys and feebly imitated by girls, under the term of "hazing."

Here is a form of conduct without the faintest justification in reason, not sanctioned by religion, under no pressure of conditions, absolutely without excuse. It is not like the merely foolish mischief done by little children, but is practised by youths and even men, sometimes with lasting injury and an occasional death. It hurts and humiliates those against whom the tormentors have no complaint. It is wanton evil, and the only explanation of it is the unchecked current of ancient custom.

Some offer in its defense the theory that it strengthens the sufferer to bear his ordeal manfully, an idea which goes back to the "pain economy" of savagery. Because much suffering was sure to befall man, endurance was a necessary virtue. To acquire it beforehand the savages underwent endurance tests—a custom wise enough in their stage of evolution. We have record of the same practice among the ancient Spartans, the "hardening" process, the youth throwing two spears at once, that one spear might seem light to him. In modern instance we see the batter swing two bats, for the same reason.

But whatever endurance may have been developed among savages by their self-inflicted injuries, the modern business man does not have to meet such trials. And it is hard to see how the absurd and outrageous inflictions of hazing can develop anything of value.

These are minor instances, but clear ones, showing undeniably the long, dribbling stream of ancient customs which filters down through the generations until definite action of enlightened understanding puts a stop to it.

It would seem possible to convince even a child of ten that it was silly to do a thing merely because one's remote ancestors did it, and that a person persisting in unreasonable conduct resembles an idiot. Children are rational if rationally treated, sometimes even if not. It is the lack of reason among those who teach them which is responsible for the persistence of primeval habits. When grown persons continue to allow the "morals" of antiquity to slide down the generations through their own conduct, we can hardly expect them to teach reason and self-control to their children.

Best proof of the absence of intelligence and the powerlessness of religion in "morals" is in our common limitation and application of the word. An "immoral" man or woman, in common parlance, is one who does not conform to our standards in the sex relation. These standards antedate both law and religion, as is shown in the masculine "moral" by which a husband may slay his wife's lover. This "unwritten law" overrides both the laws he has written against murder and the religious commandment, "Thou shalt not kill."

No field of conduct shows more conspicuously the interplay of forces which modify our behavior. The easy preëminence of "morals" so applied, proves how deeply rooted in our racial life lie the sex taboos, the basis of so much otherwise unexplainable. We see in this derivation the force of natural instinct, the influence of conditions, the restrictions of law, the slow amelioration due to education, the interference of religion, and the mere dead weight of custom.

If all these may be for the moment ignored, what would a trained intelligence recommend as "right" or "wrong" in sex relation? Surely we should demand as right such conduct as would tend to the improvement of the race and the happiness of the individual; and brand as wrong such conduct as had a reverse influence. Lacking such applied intelligence, we find the most amusingly absurd, the most abominably injurious conduct carried on age after age, despite conspicuous ill effects, so conspicuous that societies have suffered, sickened, and died under them, giving way before healthier people.

It is not at all strange that the untrammeled gropings of early thinkers should have postulated a devil to account for man's behavior. It certainly did not seem as if he could have been so foolish of his own impulse; nor was he, so far as conscious decision was used. The major trouble with all our conduct is the absence of that decision; we drift rudderless in the current of race heredity, blown here and there by winds of changing circumstance.

We assumed a thing to be right because it was customary; we believed it is right because some one told us so; and if we ever dared to question or criticize we had no sufficient knowledge on which to base better judgment. Therefore we find, in this one department of human conduct, customs ranging from vices which destroy the race to virtues which prevent its being born.

As a negative evil, the peculiar virtue of celibacy is one of the silliest we have ever produced —not under the head of morals, it is true, but through religion. Here is a function of primal importance, more so than self-preservation, the individual often being sacrificed to the continuance of the species; a function which men misused until they could see something of the harm they had done. Then they solemnly decided that the function was wrong, that the highest virtue required the abrogation of such natural duty—as if gluttony and indigestion proved that it was wrong to eat.

Under the influence of this grotesque idea we have removed from parentage some of our choicest spirits, those capable of the self-control so sadly needed by the race, leaving it to be replenished by the more indulgent. The evil is not a great one, for there never were many persons affected by it, but it is a perfect proof of what may be done under the influence of an absurd idea. Against it, thriving under all morality, is the opposite theory, that there is virtue, manly virtue, in excess.

This is due not to religion, at least to any beyond our dark beginnings, but simply to the dominance of the male. It was inevitable that he should exalt his function and attribute virtue to its performance. A world managed by women would have done the same thing for their functions, but these, being of broader application to world-service, could not have done so much harm. Giving birth, being a slow and laborious process, by no means painless, could not have been practised more than once a year at most, however honored and admired. Excesses in physical motherhood are not common enough to show much ill result, and at worst, would be self-eliminating—leading to the extinction of the exhausted mother and her perhaps enfeebled off-spring. The later processes of human motherhood—care, service, education—are of world-advantage.

The essential wrong in the masculine side of the question is in man's divorcing his share in the process from its initial purpose, using it as a pleasurable exercise, and holding it to be a proof of superiority.

Had women remained free, this in itself could have done little harm. The female is always the arbiter in the matter, if able to choose. She has her own times and seasons, and in a natural state no male can compel her at other times.

Even with the monogamous animals we do not

find the least tendency toward the irrelevant excesses which distinguish us. But man, with a female dependent on him for food, shelter, everything, could and did indulge as he chose.

The early results were terrible, leading to the extermination of many tribes which mistreated their women beyond the life limit. In quite modern history we see again the success of more chaste barbarians over the weakened and diseased older civilizations.

Surviving peoples had to work out a morality which at least would allow them to live, and they did so. Such as we have now secures the reproduction of the race by protecting some women, to some extent; and allows the excesses of men by sacrificing other women to unfruitful usage.

Against this deep-seated masculine demand religion has clamored in vain, common sense has had no power, and custom, the base of our morality, has not opposed, but condoned and sanctioned.

These effects are easy to understand, but what is not so simple and is far more discreditable, is the attitude of the thinker, and the action of the law. He who long possessed all the education there was, training his own mind in logic and contending that women had no minds to train, knowing perfectly that the sacrifice of a certain percentage of women to abnormal uses was to accommodate him, and that many of them suffered and died horribly because of it, or lived to a hideous and despised old age—he turned and blamed them for it.

Because some women, necessarily inheriting from their progenitors the excessive appetite which results from over-used functions, are themselves inclined to such suicidal life, he has failed to observe that "the market" has never been willingly filled but has always been supplied by force and fraud; or he has ignored the fact.

He liked them young; most of them are young, and do not live to grow old. The law, which requires a girl to be of a certain age before she is given power of choice for legal marriage, long allowed mere children the same choice in an illegal union. In our own country it is only within a few years, under the most strenuous efforts of women, that "the age of consent," in some states, has been raised to equal the age of legal marriage.

Once in this miserable position, there was no escape for the woman. Under the pressure of our "morality," this particular offense was considered far more wicked in the sufferer than in him who required the wickedness as a "social necessity." The law, made and enforced by men, influenced by morality far more than by religion, has continually punished the woman for doing what men wished and often forced her to do.

An act which must be mutual, which in the statute-book is forbidden to both, entails, as a matter of fact, virtually no punishment for that half-offender who is male. So deep-seated is this perverse, irrational judgment that even now, when we have learned of the results in disease from our evil habits, we seek in all ways to protect the man rather than the woman.

It is she who is "regulated," examined by compulsion, shut up till she is "safe"—for him. He, who is free to go and come, who can and does carry the worst of infections to a perfectly innocent wife and, most dreadful of all, to his unborn children—he is not segregated, examined, and imprisoned till he is "safe."

What we are here pointing out is that this state of things, so discreditable to our religion, our intelligence, and our laws, is maintained under the predominant influence of age-old "morality." Our religion, old as it is, and man-influenced as it is, is justice and liberality compared with our morals. There is nothing in the Bible to show that this particular sin is wickeder than other sins, or that the woman is to be blamed for it with such enormous disproportion.

Jesus was far more gentle with the Magdalene, and with the woman taken in adultery, than he was with the scribes, Pharisees, hypocrites he so condemned. But we, in spite of law, religion, and any sense of justice, continue to blame and punish the woman for acts but lightly disparaged in a man.

Just at present, among certain extremely modern and sophisticated persons, there is a tendency to admire promiscuity in both sexes, and to indulge in it with no sense of wrong-doing, but that has nothing to do with "morality." We must study it in the influence of philosophy on conduct.

The moral standards are very old, and still hold sway over most of the world. Only a few years ago a case came up in a New York court wherein a servant was convicted of stealing. She admitted her fault, with tears, but appealed to the judge with the singular plea that she was "an honest woman."

"I believe you," said the judge, compassionately, and gave the thief a light sentence on account of her "honesty." Fancy a young man confessing to theft, but urging in defense that he was a virgin! Even if his chastity had been admitted as evidence of "previous good character," it would hardly have been called honesty.

As a matter of fact this one virtue was for long the principal one demanded of women, and to this day there are many idle, selfish, untruthful, slanderous, extravagant women who feel perfectly virtuous because free from unchastity. Also, those who know them best find many virtues, notably kindness and generosity, among women who have lost their "virtue."

The truth at bottom of our deep horror of

unmonogamous behavior in women lies in biological law, and should be studied further under Ethics.

In contrast to the virtue required of women and not of men, we find in our common morality another one required of men and not of women. It is a virtue of deep importance, of the highest value in the maintenance and improvement of human life, the lack of which is most injurious —courage.

It is not mentioned in our religious or legal codes, but historic experience has planted it deep in our morality, for men.

It was not wanted in women. Women were expected to be meek, modest, and submissive. The very terms describing the attribute have different weight and meaning as applied to the sexes.

Liberty is a sacred thing to men; to women "a liberty" has quite a different sound. "Be bold," we encourage the boy, but to be bold was a term of reproach for the girl or woman, until our present-day indecencies. This particular field of behavior offers another interesting illustration of the conflicting currents which govern human conduct.

Circumstances develop courage in a species that survives by conquest, while the lack of it is developed in a species that survives by submission. In our peculiar kind we have reared a tangled, inconsistent race by developing courage in one sex and cowardice in the other.

No man would try to breed race-horses by crossing Arabs with Percherons, or watch-dogs by mixture of the spaniel and the bull. Yet he has cheerfully expected to develop his own species by the constant crossing of courage and cowardice.

Women are not ashamed of being cowards. They will own to it without a blush, even, indeed, with a sort of pride, knowing it to be a valued secondary sex character which pleases men. As a man is not ashamed of licentiousness which would be ruin to a woman, so a woman is not ashamed of cowardice which would utterly disgrace a man.

Looking down a list of our commonly accepted virtues, it is clear that morality requires more of them, or a higher degree of them, of women than of men. Of women especially have been required the convenient virtues of a subject class: obedience, patience, endurance, contentment, humility, resignation, temperance, prudence, industry, kindness, cheerfulness, modesty, gratitude, thrift, and unselfishness.

Of men we have required fewer; and those of a different nature: courage, truth, justice, loyalty to one another, generosity, patriotism, and honor. In the morality of men is a code which forbids one to betray another's vices or diseases to a woman, though it be to save her. Truth is little enough upheld by either sex, but a man is supposed to "keep his word," where a woman is allowed to "change her mind." Justice, as far as we have any, is sustained by men, even while they do such unmeasured injustice. (This was called a free country while yet slavery existed, and a democracy while half the people had no vote.) Generosity was necessarily confined to the class which held the purse; a man takes pride in being "a free spender" where a woman is praised for thrift.

As to honor, that peculiar creation of the

mind of man needs special emphasis. In its dim beginnings it doubtless comes from the natural pride of the male. As formulated by the early savage, it found expression in distinctive decorations, notably in head ornaments, and with increase of power his pride was gratified by formulæ of prostration and fine words. With special growth all this deepened and widened till we have something quite outside the range of any other creature, a whole field of ambition and benefit consisting in "honor" only—in being set one above another and bowed down to, with a vast array of titles to mark distinction.

And such honor, for all the ages, was for man alone; save, indeed, where priestesses and queens by marriage shared in his glories to some degree. The whole long list of titles and distinctions, of "orders" and decorations, were almost altogether his. Only as his "lady" did woman share in lordship, or as his daughter, perhaps. We hear of the "queen mother," but not of the "king father"; man was king in himself.

With these external honors, grew up, within, an accompanying spirit. We begin to hear of "my knightly honor," and of "the honor of a gentleman." It is the spirit called "honor" which is so peculiarly male, and also peculiar in other ways. Women, to be sure, had their "honor," but that was merely their chief virtue, chastity; and, strangely enough, it could be taken from them by force. A man might be killed, imprisoned, or tortured by his enemy, but a woman could be "dishonored."

The man's honor partook of this precarious character only when it was lodged in the keeping of another, his wife. If she committed adultery it dishonored him, but if he did it, it did not dishonor her. When she lost her honor, she lost his into the bargain; but his own honor, not inhering in her particular virtue, was not so imperiled by any deed of his.

In the meandering course of masculine morals the word "honor" finds strange uses. We have spoken already of that ticklish honor which was hopelessly endangered by a glove flung in the face, and triumphantly reëstablished by pistol-shot or sword-thrust in reply. The "affair of honor" must needs be conducted with great ceremony and politeness, two "seconds," and a surgeon.

But there is another extreme of masculine morality which is still more quaint,—that wherein sums wagered in gambling become "debts of honor." Debts owed one's tailor, or the tradesmen who furnished food for the household might be ignored without blame; unpaid servants, even a wife or a child in need, might go neglected, but the debt of "honor" must be paid.

This field of social eccentricity is not so important as that previously discussed, but is an equally clear proof of the disconnection between morality and ethics, or morality and common sense.

CHAPTER VIII

ETHICS AND CONDUCT

THIS title is somewhat like "Navigation and the Sailing of a Ship," or "Agriculture and Farming."

Ships were sailed, to be sure, before navigation was learned, but the science of navigation promotes the safe and swift passage of ships. Farming, also, can be carried on with almost no knowledge of agriculture, with lamentable results to the soil and to the farmer, but our agricultural colleges are of vast assistance in improving the condition of both.

Ethics is the science of conduct; that's all. It should be the commonest, easiest, most practical of sciences. Every child should have his first lessons in ethics much before those in arithmetic or geography. There is nothing of such immediate importance as knowing how to behave—and behaving as we know how.

Of course we strive to produce what we consider desirable conduct in children, but not with any reference to ethics. As far as most of us know, ethics is a science with a large S, a thing to be studied by advanced classes in college, like Quaternions.

Here is the child, whose actions spring first from inherited impulses, secondly from his environment, thirdly from imitation, fourthly, and most important, from his own judgment and will. As we are seldom satisfied with the result of the first three influences, as we cannot alter his inheritance, nor, usually, his environment, as we distinctly do not wish him to imitate us, and do not know how to cultivate judgment and will, we apply what power we have to "make him behave."

As we have no knowledge of ethics in our own behavior, it is not surprising that we use none with him. We tell him to do this or not to do that in accordance with our own convenience, with our morality ancient and current, with our customs of class, race, or profession, with our religious beliefs, with some theory we may have adopted, with anything except ethics.

What he never learns is *why* one thing is right and another wrong, and why some things are so much more right and wrong than others.

Our ideas of right and wrong are mainly derived from our religions, while our practices of right and wrong spring principally from our morality.   In neither case have we a definite, provable knowledge of what constitutes right and wrong, fit to teach to a child.

Yet these things are no mystery.   In the case of any game we can learn easily enough the right and wrong way to play.   In running any machine, we soon find out how it is to be done rightly, or wrongly.   To any living creature it is clear that right conduct is such as is conducive to his best maintenance and improvement.

What is right for a rabbit, for instance?   To eat good food, to escape his enemies, to multiply and replenish the earth.   The rabbit does his duty and her duty, automatically, as it were. You do not see a rabbit wasting his time by endeavoring to climb trees, or in futile efforts to fly.   Being a good rabbit does not require much brain power, nor develop it.

To be a good human creature is a far more

complicated job; that is why we have brains. But brains are of little use to most of us. We go from the cradle to the grave, doing what we are told, or what other people do, or what we happen to feel like, and, to some extent, what our religion demands, without ever understanding the science of conduct.

Yet even in its later complications this is no puzzle if we study it fairly.

First there is our individual existence, wherein our virtues are those of any other animal. Then our family relationship, a part of the higher development of the reproductive processes. Then, highest and most important, our social relationship, in which lies the whole range of what we consciously apprehend as ethics.

Right and wrong, in our human sense, cannot be predicated of an individual. A man permanently isolated, can no more do wrong or right than could any other solitary animal.

It is perfectly easy to teach the animal ethics to any child; he may not be quick at it, as some are not quick at figures, but the reasons for right behavior in eating, sleeping, keeping clean and warm, and so on, are plain enough. These things should be taught from the first as being right or wrong, so that we should grow up more ashamed of a bad breath than of dirty hands, of a slouching carriage of the body than of bad table manners.

The ethics of health needs clear instruction, and its application in later matters of "morals" will be most helpful.   At present we may show a boy or a girl that such a practice will injure the health, but they attach no weight to this consequence.   In athletic development the boy becomes eager to take right exercise, but even there he will often weaken his heart for life by frantic competition, and not feel guilty.

As for girls, it is only lately and partially that the idea of right physical development has entered their heads; and in the line of their main physical duty, right motherhood, our "morality" has allowed them to grow up in complete ignorance.

The recent "style" of a hollow-chested slouch shows how little a girl knows or cares for physical integrity, or for beauty.

Family ethics is equally plain, and some of it has to be learned, in practice, at least.   Yet in many families there is no instruction in respect for one another's privacy, in courtesy from parent to child and among children; and such indefensible evils as teasing go unchecked.

The usual family discipline has no base in justice. It is arbitrary and enforced by punishments which vary, not with any ethical judgment but according to the temper and education of the parent. The two things most definitely required in our traditional family training are obedience and duty to parents—that strange invention of the governing father.

Obedience as a virtue in itself, disobedience as a sin, hold disproportionate value in our categories. The concept of "sin," adding special condemnation to an error in conduct merely because it was forbidden, has no relation to the importance of the act, only to its prohibition. Believers in some religions hold it "sin" to eat meat on one day, to play games on another, to dance, to go to the theater.

A pious old gentlemen, of the Society of Friends, reproved a lady for playing solitaire. "I do not gamble," said she, "and cards are not wrong in themselves." "Cards," he declared, "are the devil's instruments. They are used for gambling and betting, and should never be touched in any way." To which she responded, "Do you feel that way about horses?"

That good man was religious but not ethical. He never studied the science of conduct to determine why an act was right or wrong, but accepted what he was taught without a murmur. Yet that attitude of mind is itself wrong, injurious to society. Our conscious progress depends on a growing ability to distinguish ethical values in the widening range of social relationship; and this ability is not cultivated at home, at school or in church. Parent and teacher and priest agree in teaching obedience as a virtue, not in teaching the clear reasons for right doing.

Obedience is often a convenience and sometimes a necessity, but never in itself a virtue. Even in the commonest instance, that of the soldier, the deeds he commits under orders may be of the most hideous evil; witness certain acts of German soldiers in Belgium. A wrong act does not become right because some one tells you to commit it.

We were confused as to obedience because of

the nature of the first group activities of men. In the hunting-party, in warfare, and as navigation began, the signal for action must be instantly accepted. In these relationships obedience is a necessity. We may here find again the influence of retarded development in the woman. She, like the animal mother, knew only one method of guiding the young, through exacting obedience. The baby partridge who does not obey, does not "freeze" at the cry of the hawk-frightened mother, is eaten by that discerning enemy. Those who obeyed survived, and transmitted the "instinct" of prompt obedience. The human mother started with the same impulse, knew only the same method, and since she has made virtually no progress in her work, rather resisting the influence of men educators, obedience is still her chief demand, and punishment her means of compulsion.

Punishment is quite a different thing from consequences. That cancer of the tongue may follow upon too much smoking is a consequence, not a punishment. The whipping of a child for running away, or for any other "disobedience" is a punishment, not a consequence. Ethics, being a science, deals with known laws of cause and effect, not with personal orders and commandments.

The discipline of children, which gives us our first impressions of right and wrong behavior, is so crudely unreasonable as to unsettle our ethical judgments for life. The growing human mind should not be educated with methods of training suitable only to animals.

The mother bear cuffs her cub, the mother cat cuffs her kitten, and the mother human cuffs her child, under identical impulses and limitations. What the mother knows she seeks to teach her child; his conduct she has to guide for his protection, and the only methods of culture known to her are example and punishment. Example is used much—"Do it as I do,"—and is visibly effective, perhaps most so in matters not definitely taught; but punishment is the main stay; prohibitions and penalties surround our youth.

The sense of ethical distinction inevitably absorbed in infancy starts with "being good" as a baby—which consists in doing nothing. "He is such a good baby," says the admiring mother or nurse, of the child who does not cry or pull things about.   As he grows older he becomes conscious that most of the things he wants to do are "bad," and the "good" things he is told to do are not pleasant.

This is the earliest and worst of the ethical impressions given our children. Instead of learning that all our right conduct is solidly based on advantage to humanity, and that the reason a thing is wrong is because it is harmful, he grows up with the inner conviction that "being good" consists in doing what one is ordered, is largely negative, and mostly disagreeable.

Morality often agrees with this impression, and religion has stressed it deeply, adding the weight of divine authority to the orders, and the measureless concept of eternity to the rewards and penalties. Our system of law, with arbitrary punishment attached to offenses, gives further weight to such theory of conduct, and not in a lifetime, under years of spanking, years of church-going, or years in the penitentiary, do we ever learn why this conduct is right and that wrong.

Consider a simple primary offense, like stealing.

The savage, living in a free world, took what he could get, like any other animal. As soon as private property appeared, which is a condition of social relationship, as special tools, weapons, and the like, if one man took from another there was animosity, combat, and the efficiency of the tribe was impaired. Taking from another tribe was quite another matter; that is called "looting" and is still practised freely.

Private property is a social right, which may be formulated as follows: The individual has a right to those things which enable him to do his best social service.

All ethical values are based on social relations; society confers the "right" and society must defend it. But in our ethicless behavior, carrying a sub-human egotism on into human relations, we have let our "right" to private property swell into the "wrong" of private ownership of public property, setting no limit to possession. The class warfare of our troubled times makes a similar mistake, ignoring the social claim and setting up those of a "class," of certain grades of labor. The profiteer and the speculator rob society, and so do the slacker and the committer of sabotage. Stealing was wrong long before any commandment was written. It is forbidden because it is wrong, not wrong because it is forbidden.

Ethics is a social science,—*the* social science, in fact,—being a consciously apprehended system of modifying our behavior in the interests of our common happiness and progress. Ethics covers all our inter-relationship, in economics, in politics, in ordinary intercourse. Its basis is an understanding of the nature of society, its structure and functions. That conduct is right which tends to the best development of humanity; that is wrong which injures it. The relative importance, the degree of rightness or wrongness in a given act, is according to the amount of good or evil in its effect upon society.

To poison one man's food is wrong. To poison the food of the public is more wrong. To weaken and poison the public mind is worse, far worse. The results are not so instantly visible, but do more harm. That is why a man who prints lies and lewdness in his newspapers is more wicked than one who puts benzoate in his canned goods.

Here is but the merest suggestion as to the basis of ethics. In our study we seek for the effect of a too-masculine influence upon it. Nowhere is this influence more strongly in evidence than in the visible protection for man's special weaknesses, accorded to himself by the head of the family, the head of the church, and also the teacher of ethics. Once started on that study, he could but develop a large range of conduct to which ethical values were applied, but he carefully exempted one wide field, or rather two, as quite outside such restrictions: "All 's fair in love and war."

Love, so called, and war, are the essentially masculine lines of activity, and the most enjoyed. Upon their unchecked pursuit great evil to society ensued, yet they remained outside the researches of the ethicist. In the family, with its subordinate and dependent woman, its children long held to be the property of the father, even man's sense of justice was aborted. The conditions of slavery, of ownership, of authority, with the dependence and submission of the owned, check the growth of ethics completely. This dominance underlies the despotism of officer, priest, and king, and still finds expression in the attitude of our "captains of industry."

In their progressive human relationship men learned the practical basis of ethics, and developed it by degrees in widening codes of law. Such and such conduct was recognized as inimical to the public good and forbidden, other conduct, seen as beneficial, was commended, honored. The sense of right and wrong has grown with our growth, as it must, but most unevenly.

If women also had entered into that social relationship which is as proper to them as to men, our ethical sense could not have been so one-sided. They lived only in the family relationship, which condition is by no means peculiar to humanity. Other animals have families but not patriarchal families; and when they live in groups their social life is either wholly feminine, as with ants and bees, or comprises both sexes.

Our family with the male head has established authority, and carried it on in larger relations. Keeping cattle and keeping slaves, having huge families of both in which he was absolute lord, he grew more and more to demand obedience. The growing power of the priesthood demanded obedience. The prophets, appealing from priest to deity, demanded obedience. The kings, becoming more and more powerful as vast empires developed, demanded obedience. The law, slowly rising even over the king, demanded obedience. To believe and to obey—these have been given highest place in our ethics.

But the free use of one's mind, as essential to mental health as is physical exercise to the body; and the strong use of one's will, absolute requisite of self-governed conduct—these were not encouraged by slave-mother nor master-father. See how far stretches the use of authority and punishment in that great social engine, the law. Here is command, thou shalt and thou shalt not. Here is punishment for disobedience. And here is not the faintest movement toward teaching people the laws they are expected to obey. Can we imagine convocations of mothers solemnly enacting laws for their children to follow and never telling them anything about it—punishing them for infraction of laws they never heard of, with the solemn proclamation, "Ignorance is no excuse in the eyes of the law"?

Against a wholly masculine dominance has slowly and with infinite difficulty uprisen the human spirit, which is neither masculine nor feminine, and which is, by nature, reasonable. Now we are just beginning to exercise those race qualities by which it is possible for us to learn what is right conduct for the human race and in some degree so to live.

Ethics, as we have seen, is a social science. Its basis and its laws are all inter-personal. Every human virtue is in relationship among people; it cannot be practised alone. Love, truth, honesty, generosity, efficiency in service, or hate, falsehood, dishonesty, cruelty, malingerings, and sabotage—there is nothing in the field of ethical science that is not a matter of social relationship.

So far, in our masculine world, but one general ethical concept has been established in social relationship; that is what we call patriotism. This is a true virtue and of deep importance. But, alas! it was sadly curtailed by the usual male limitations. Sweet and proper they called it that a man should die for his country—always death in the foreground, always fighting as the chief service.

Meanwhile the discoverer, the inventor, the teacher, the artist, the craftsman of every sort, and, under all, the farmer and drover who feed us—these lived for their country, without any recognition as patriots, even from themselves.

Sweet and proper it is that every human being should be reared from babyhood to clear realization of the great social body to which he belongs, and of the fact that his highest duty is the service of that society. There are times when this service has to be by fighting, as the early settler had to leave the plow for the gun to protect his family from wolves or savages. But the living for his family would have been a poor one if his duty had stopped with shooting. It is in the specialized and organized services by which the world lives, in the work we do, in our business relations that human duty lies most clear, and yet here, so far, neither religion, morality, nor ethics has made us "good."

CHAPTER IX

PHILOSOPHY AND CONDUCT

A COUNTRY boy of eleven, tramping through the snow to visit his snares and traps, says over and over to tagging little sister: "I don't expect to find anything. I don't expect to find anything." He had learned that the less one anticipates the less one is disappointed, while success is all the pleasanter if unexpected. That is philosophy.

"There is no use in crying over spilt milk." "It's dogged that does it." "Honesty is the best policy." "A stitch in time saves nine." All the practical maxims of popular proverbs are parts of philosophy, a natural product of the human mind.

The capacity to perceive abstractions, to generalize, to observe and remember and collate impressions, and to substitute some generalization for repeated experiment—this is the basis of philosophy. It was limited, simple, and most practical at first, but with our growing mental powers we have developed elaborate systems of philosophy so complicated and abstract as to be followed only by studious minds.

The self-torturing savage is the precursor of the Stoic Philosophy; the self-indulgent savage, of the Epicurean. The submissive and long-oppressed Oriental produces his philosophy of Fatalism; the Englishman and his American descendant make a philosophy of resistance and progress, crying, "Never say die!" and "You can't keep a good man down!" The morbid, woman-hating Schopenhauer gives us a philosophy of grisly pessimism, followed to a worse degree by Nietzsche. In more modern times we have the pragmatic philosophy of William James, and the more esoteric work of Bergson. Philosophies change more widely and rapidly than religions, and, obviously, they cannot all be true.

All are examples of the mental process by which one dominant idea tends to bring out derivative ideas, and, if applicable to human conduct, influences the behavior of the race. As that behavior is our strongest modifying condition, it becomes extremely important that our philosophy be sound.

Every religion is strongly tinctured with the prevalent philosophy of its people; the same religion, spreading over different races, changes widely, according to their previous ideas.

It is specially important, therefore, to learn what popular philosophies have contributed to our man-interpreted religions, to our laws, our morals, our general behavior, that they should one and all have so far failed to improve the world as they ought.

That very ancient theory best known as Stoic, is seen trickling down the ages to such late expression as Longfellow's "Learn how sublime a thing it is to suffer and be strong." We have not yet grasped the idea that it is foolish to suffer if one can help it, much better to be strong without the suffering. At the suggestion, up rises the old philosophy of a primitive pain-economy, and we are told that it is suffering which develops strength.

When we want strength in our draft-horses do we cultivate it by abusing them? Strength is developed by exercise, not by suffering; yet so pervasive is this miserable relic of early thought, that in some great religions it holds high place, and we assume an essential virtue in having a hard time. It permeates our common economic theories, as shown in the generally accepted belief that there is some developing influence in poverty and deprivation.

All the experience of ages of farming and breeding animals shows that if we wish to cultivate and improve a living thing we must protect it from enemies and competitors, and supply its needs to the best of our ability. In practice, with our own children, we seek to do the same thing, quite rightly. But the false philosophy, so deeply implanted in our minds, still governs our ideas, and, alas! our actions. If it were not for this ancient folly, no civilized race would bear the glaring evils of unnecessary poverty.

We have a quite general conviction that there is essential good in doing right under difficulties, whereas the virtue is in the act, according to its consequences, not according to its difficulties. We boast of "the sweet uses of adversity," of character developed by hardship, as a small boy boasts of a stone-bruise or a blister.

It is this which has helped to mislead us in the Christian religion, diverting our minds from what Jesus taught that we should do, to the incidents of his suffering and sacrifice by which we hoped to profit. Whereas, if Jesus had been gladly accepted and obeyed, had lived on to a grand old age, had married and left children, the truths which he taught would have been exactly as valuable.

The Epicurean philosophy, with its frank Hedonism, though far more closely allied to our natural impulses, has never made much headway against Stoicism and Fatalism. These doctrines of suffering and submission have had tremendous weight, because of the amount of self-made misery we had to bear, and of our long helplessness in slavery.

A given society seems to generate a philosophy as an anti-toxin to the diseased conditions it endures, and each religion is colored thereby. We hear much of "The consolations of religion," never of its congratulations. We send for the priest at sick-bed and death-bed, not for the birthday or "coming-out" party. The Hebrews, finding it impossible to reconcile their position as

God's chosen people with their grievous misfortunes, developed, as Santayana has so clearly shown, their pet philosophy—"Whom the Lord loveth, he chasteneth." What the Oriental calls Kismet we call the will of God, preaching the same submission. Submission is pushed so far in that acrobatic pyramid of thought called Calvinism that we were taught we must be willing to be damned—for the glory of God! Why should so much mental activity have stopped there, and not inquired what glory there was in an omnipotent being torturing forever a puny little creature who could in no way defend himself? Would it be to the glory of a man to fry ants?

Dominant early thinkers, being men, and having in their minds as premises the common errors as to the nature and power of women, naturally incorporated these errors in their systems of philosophy. What the women thought, is not recorded, any more than the lion has erected a statue to the victor in the hunt.

So we find little but condemnation and abuse of women, perhaps strongest in the German philosophy of Schopenhauer. A belated example of such ancient attitude of mind is found in a very young German Jew, one Otto Weininger, who published a book some twenty years ago, entitled "Sex and Character." In this he re-embodied many primitive ideas about women, and arranged them in a definite philosophy of their relation to life.   Women, according to this youth (he was under twenty-one as I remember, and shot himself before he grew much older) had no souls, no minds, no memory, no ideas.   The only distinctive quality he accorded them was a tendency to match-making!   "Woman," he said "is the visible embodiment of man's sins."   His book went through many editions in Germany, and was widely translated.

Quite aside from the fruits of special thinkers, we may trace this influence even more conspicuously in that popular philosophy expressed in proverbs.   Long before reading and writing were common, the ordinary convictions of a people were expressed in saws and sayings, spread wide by repetition and handed down from one generation to the next.

A proverb becomes such only through wide acceptance and long usage.   Nothing so con-

clusively proves popular opinion as to find it pro-
verbially expressed.

After study of a compendium of such lore,
"Proverbs of All Races," an analysis was made
of the difference between the general ideas as to
men and as to women.   The first distinction lay
in the very few proverbs about women as compared with the bulk of the collection, which was
about men.   The next distinction lay in this,
that whereas those about men were qualified, as
"A fat man," "A rich man," "A wise man," and
so on, the others almost without exception spoke
simply of "A woman."   The third distinction
was painfully clear: the great mass of world
opinion about women was overwhelmingly bad,
contemptuous and derogatory to a degree:

Men are deeds and women are words;

A man of straw is worth a woman of gold;

Man, woman, and the devil are the three degrees of
comparison;

Whoso hath an eel by the tail and a woman by her
word hath a slippery handle;

Whoso loseth his wife and a farthing hath great loss
in the farthing;

A dead wife's the best goods in a man's house;
As much pity to see a woman weep as to see a goose
go barefoot.

One or two proverbs spoke approvingly of a "good" wife, and there was just one in the whole book which seemed to uncover hidden depths of rebellion: "That char is well charred, as the goodwife said when she hanged her husband."

"Goodwife" is here, probably, a mere title, not a term of approbation.

Our conduct, always influenced by ideas, has been heavily modified by this tremendous weight of world opinion; not all the facts of life could counterbalance it. Our philosophy, both esoteric and popular, has shown the effects of masculine thought and feeling, based on incorrect premises. No protest from the submerged sex had any force to check it. Did woman argue, she was told, "A continual dropping on a very rainy day and a contentious woman are alike," and that was all the satisfaction she got.

In the phenomena of our present life the influence of philosophy is just as evident, and still for the most part expresses the masculine view. Most conspicuous and most evil in its immediate expression in conduct, is the perverted sex-philosophy of Freud and his followers.

This seems to embody the last effort on the part of man to maintain his misuse of the female. Her growing freedom under the law has robbed him of his "rights" in this line; the wiser interpretation of religion repudiates such Oriental dicta as "Her desire shall be unto her husband and he shall rule over her"; economic independence enables a woman to live at another price than sex-submission; better understanding of laws of health shows that frequent sex-indulgence is by no means a necessity, as once maintained, but an injury; and, best of all, biology now teaches that the female throughout nature is the sole arbiter in the sex relation and never requires it save for its real purpose.

With the change in the attitude of "good women," and with a new interest in the protection of ignorant young girls from exploitation, the supply no longer met the demand. It was natural enough that the mind of man should evolve a philosophy of sex calculated to meet his desires, and, as a philosophy, serenely indifferent to facts.

This does not require an overt act. Such a product is as unconsciously developed as were the theories of fatalism, of submission, of the advantage of bad conditions. Under pressure the mind can usually work out a justifying theory which will seem as real to the producer as a hand-made idol to its worshipper.

Freud's morbid philosophy assumes sex to be the mainspring of life, and almost the whole of it, some small allowance being made for the needs of the stomach.

Sex, according to Freud, dominates the sensations even of a nursing baby, whose satisfaction, even when it is being fed at the mother's breast, he calls "sexual"! A species of biological blasphemy, this; an idea so revolting to a healthy mind as to cause nausea. But by such philosophy it is quite easily accepted, and not considered in any way objectionable, for in it Sex is Life and most of our actions from the cradle to the grave are prompted by Sex.

Not since the phallic religions of antiquity has sex-worship so strongly appeared. Its teachers, being forced to recognize the appalling results of extreme over-indulgence, that corner is turned by a recommendation to "sublimate" sex, turning its energies into other channels. But whatever you wish to do—invent, discover, decorate, sing, dance, act, paint, manufacture, teach—the power that urges you is called sex energy.

There is a fallacious ingenuity in the position. One might conceivably attribute all we do to our art instinct, to a religious instinct, to some obscure urge from the liver or spleen; there would be no denying it. For you may confront the Freudian with the gallant achievements of a racing gelding, and the reply is, "Yes, denied normal expression, his sex energy is so manifested." Stallion, mare, or gelding—the power which makes them run is still called sex!

In its normal degree and right relationship sex is as good as any other natural force. In unnatural over-development and misuse it is as objectionable as acromegaly.

That the male, originated for sex use, should overestimate the importance of his raison d'etre is natural. But that the human female, the race type, having the main responsibility for the im-

provement of humanity, should accept any such
swollen assumption of importance in her early
assistant, is absurd.

The immense superiority of men over women
in human advancement has not the faintest connection with their sex.   On the contrary, their
preoccupation with sex, their surrender to its impulses, has been a hindrance and a detriment to
human progress.

A human philosophy such as we shall develop
when the true race type has learned its power and
duty, will express itself both in systematic
thought and in popular sayings, resting on facts
like these:

Living things are urged by three natural
forces, the tendency to self-preservation, to race-
preservation, and to improvement.

Under the first the race keeps alive, under the
second it is reproduced, under the third it
develops.

All surviving races have kept alive, and have
reproduced; many have developed, some far
more than others.

The human race has developed more highly

than any other, and among different peoples some excel others in their degree of humanness.

Human development is largely conscious, increasing as we become able to understand what conditions benefit us and how to apply them more widely, as, for instance, in education.

In surveying the field of life below and behind us, we see that some of the lower forms are stronger in self-preservation than higher ones, as certain rotifers can sustain degrees of heat or cold which would kill a horse; and also that sex plays a larger proportionate part in the lower than in the higher stages of development. In many forms the male lives only long enough to fertilize the female, or the females live only long enough to reproduce themselves; and the more helpless the creature is, the more there are of its progeny, as in the three-million-egged oyster.

As race-improvement developed more varied and powerful creatures, able to secure their lives without incessant effort, and to protect and nourish their young, the sex processes dwindle in relative importance. When we reach the highest orders of mammalia,—the monogamous carnivora, for instance,—we find a life union with periodic pairing, and a limited number of young.

The most casual survey of physical evolution shows it as a process of change, growth, development, filling the world with its vast variety of forms, vegetable and animal.

The most casual survey of social evolution shows it to be a process of growth and change, not along lines of reproductive activity, in which the rabbit is easily our leader, but in racial functions, in the trades and crafts, in art, in science, in government, in education, in religion. These are not functions of sex, nor in any way attributable to it. It is possible to *say* they are, just as many earnest persons attribute our advanced civilization to Christianity, regardless of the fact that the Abyssinians also are Christians.

It is easy to see that if Christianity is the cause of a given condition, then that condition will be found where people are Christians and be absent where they are not. Yet Russia is Christian, Ireland is Christian, Spain is Christian, Germany is Christian. The difference in their conditions must be due to other causes.

So with this alleged stimulus of sex, all people have it; some have far more of it than others. If human achievements are produced by sex, we have a right to expect all great men to be highly sexed and all highly sexed men to be great. But this is most patently not the case; witness the powerful influence on their time of both Ruskin and Carlyle, men sadly lacking in this particular; and witness the failure to produce anything worth while to humanity by many a lusty Don Juan.

Philosophy, in this man's world, has been heavily modified by sex, and never more so than in the belated revival of phallic worship so solemnly advanced by Freud.

"Life's fitful fever" will not seem so fitful nor so feverish when the sounder thought of the more human female begins to make itself felt.

It is pleasant to imagine some new proverbs, from her side:

What hurts the mother hurts the race.
A cook, a nurse, and a teacher are not the same thing.
A baby is more important than a corpse.
'T is a weak man that needs a whole woman to wait on him.

What's sauce for the gander is sauce for the goose.
Spend on the school and save on the prison.
Make fewer laws and keep more.
I love you, said the pig to the pudding.

A rational and strengthening philosophy of life will come to us through thinking motherhood.   It is time.

CHAPTER X

RELIGION AND CONDUCT

WE come here to a more particular study of one of the main positions of this book: that our conscious conduct may be and often is modified by ideas; that these ideas or concepts are frequently found to have a more powerful influence on conduct than inherited tendency or the effect of environment; and among all such influences that of the group of concepts forming a religion is the strongest.

Something has been shown of the effect of our ordinary morals and customs upon conduct, and also of our vague and limited perceptions in philosophy. It is not possible to avoid a more or less constant reference to the male influence, because it is under that influence that our previous world has been developed. In religion especially, this masculinity is continually apparent, but in the present chapter the intention is to dwell on the power of religious concepts of any sort as affecting conduct, apart from those peculiarly masculine.

No exhaustive research is required, merely reference to certain well-known requirements in some of the most commonly known religions. Let us look at these as they have modified our conduct in regard to those three laws of living, self-preservation, race-preservation, and improvement.

As to self-preservation, three of our greatest religions work directly against this primal impulse, this most necessary and useful impulse. In Buddhism we find the first "sublime truth" set forth as follows: "All existence is evil, because all existence is subject to change and decay." So far from defending themselves, the Buddhists teach non-resistance and self-sacrifice more successfully than do Christians. Their devotees renounce all personal desires, live by sheer beggary, offer their lives for others—even for animals.

This is to some degree paralleled by the Christian teaching of renunciation and self-sacrifice, though it has never been carried out by

Christians as generally as by Buddhists. Still, the Christian doctrine of taking no thought for the morrow, and of the forgiveness of enemies, has had enough influence upon conduct frequently to controvert the impulse of self-preservation.

In the evolution of ideas, we may clearly mark the early self-torture theory growing on through the ages, widening into mild doctrines of patience, endurance, resignation, and contentment; or intensifying to the boundless heroics of the self-made martyr. This is interesting enough as a matter of research, but as affecting the progress of the race it is lamentable.

Once the duty of improvement is recognized, we see also the error of contentment. If all life is a horrid mistake, then it is right enough to try to escape from it, as does Buddhist or Brahman. If it is bad and hopeless, but our duty to endure to the end, then it is, of course, right to preach and practise contentment. But if life is a growing thing, if we and our world are capable of endless improvement and able to promote it, we should never be contented.

The depth and breadth of the effect of the

evolutionary concept upon religion has not yet been apprehended. It is quite rationally opposed as a contradiction of accepted religious traditions, and as shaking our acceptance of ancient legends as "the word of God." It was not seen as a new underlying law of ethics, a new recognition of the nature of life, and so calling for a revaluation of all our standards.

In many religions, truth has been held a virtue, but their truth was something finished and not to be questioned. To the student of natural law, truth is something never finished and always calling for further inquiry. Such an attitude could not be encouraged by any revealed religion.

Courage to face facts, to take up new knowledge, to outgrow old habits—such a virtue could not be very heartily endorsed by those whose first requirements were belief, submission, obedience. Fortunately for us, the natural laws of social evolution were stronger, even, than the commands of any faith.

The wide and rapid progress of certain so-called "Christian" nations, is by no means to be traced to their Christianity, but to most un-Christian activities in eagerly providing for the morrow and laying up for themselves treasures upon earth.

So far as religion has modified our conduct in this line, it is in exact opposition to the urge toward self-preservation. The Armenians, for instance, are Christians, of a singularly unresisting and apparently forgiving nature, but the unspeakable Turk has pretty nearly exterminated them. The other Christians, continually forgiving the Turk, have made no improvement in him, and have not, meanwhile, benefited the Armenians save in temporary and partial "relief."

It may be that the Armenians will profit in a future life by their non-resistance, but it has certainly not helped in self-preservation here. It may be said, of course, that in the case of a non-resistant people their non-resistance is developed not by religious teaching but by the effect of ages of survival through that process. Rabbits survive without further efforts at self-preservation than to eat what they can and produce young in ceaseless numbers, yet in Australia they are a menace worse than wolves. Locusts do not fight, yet they do more mischief by their peaceful penetration than if they were all hornets. Small, tough, greedy, and prolific creatures are harder to escape than big ones not so numerous.   In some South American villages the human inhabitants have been completely overcome and driven out by ants.   So it might fairly be held that the doctrine of non-resistance is only a subtler method of conquest, in which case it loses much of its emotional appeal.

More widely potent than the teaching of non-resistance, and possibly underlying it in the evolution of ideas, is that fundamental error before referred to called fatalism.   This seems to have been the negative comfort of suffering races under evils they were unable to combat.   In its application among Hindus, we find a private self-made fate called "karma."

"Karma," said Buddha, "is the most essential property of all beings; it is inherited from previous births; it is the cause of all good and evil, and the reason why some are mean and some exalted when they come into the world."   Consider the effect of such a doctrine upon the progress of the human race; its discouragement of effort, its indifference to the sufferings of others.

Buddhism sprang from Brahmanism, and

Brahmanism, in all its three philosophies, postulates the transmigration of the individual soul from body to body in successive births, and calls this continuous reappearance "an evil resultant from desire." It is an amazing proof of the capacities of the human mind that sentient beings, belonging to the most powerful of all species, have evolved as their basic concept in three great religions the strange idea that life is an evil, and that we cannot help it, except by negativing all natural impulses. Using the very power which fatalism denies, the pious Brahman "lives destitute of passions and affections." The unescapable evils of living are, after all, to be dodged by the simple device of not living; by using all our high preëminence in reason and will to form false concepts and so act upon them as to oppose every natural instinct. Such prodigious proof of our power consciously to modify conduct is given by the races most wholly accepting fatalism. The effect of their doctrine upon human conduct, if not fully successful in transplanting all believers from this existence into the other life they seek, is at least successful in making their behavior visibly different from that of Mohammedans, for instance, even of the same race.

In regard to the next great primal law, race-preservation, we again find amazing concepts of religion opposing, injuring, and sometimes preventing that process. Among other animals, the maternal instinct, sometimes accompanied by paternal assistance, was sufficient to maintain the race. With us, a conscious recognition of that compelling necessity found expression in the concept of parental duty. Here reasoned action works with and helps nature. If the father failed in his duty, both law and public opinion forced him to compliance.

But religion, at an early stage, set up a new duty, having no parallel in nature—the duty of children to parents. This peculiar inversion of a natural relation has gone to strange lengths, as in the extreme of ancestor-worship, and in such sacrificial acts as the Japanese daughter selling herself to benefit her parents.

Christianity does not go so far as that, but it does encourage a girl, to renounce all natural life for herself, as love, marriage, children, even industrial independence, in order to devote herself to the personal care and service of one or both parents. Frequently the dutiful girl is left a middle-aged orphan, thwarted in all functions, both individual and social, and is called "a good daughter."

Such behavior, if universal, would promptly extinguish the human race, and so can hardly be justified in ethics. But its prevalence among millions of peoples following several faiths, shows again the power of religion over conduct, even when the duty demanded requires the suppression of the strongest natural desire.

In regard to sex in its general use as a pleasure, apart from reproduction, religion, exalting celibacy, has again been potent in enabling us to resist not only a natural impulse but an exaggerated one. The early recognition, by men, of the visible evil produced by their excessive indulgence, resulted in a reaction which assumed a special virtue in total abstinence: as the evils of drunkenness have resulted in prohibition, which temperate people never need.

Man's utter contempt for the class of women he well called "unfortunate," yet who were maintained by purchase, force, and fraud for what he termed "a necessity," led to the exaltation of virginity as a virtue. A clean, natural function being perverted and debased, failure to exercise it was then called "holy." This strange concept has been quite generally adopted in several religions, and has resulted in a celibate priesthood, and groups of "sacred virgins" in connection with temple worship. While celibacy has never been attained to the full degree urged by religion, there has been enough of it to prove once more the power of concept upon conduct.

In our general lines of enjoyment is shown strong evidence of this force. In nature we find all conscious creatures led by pleasure and warned by pain. The essential processes of living are either unconsciously performed, as breathing, digesting, and the like, or are attended by pleasure, as eating, drinking, and mating. Human beings, becoming able to apprehend pleasure as a concept, either pursued it as an end in itself without regard to the process it was meant to serve, or assumed it be in itself an evil.

Eating, for instance, is as common, as natural, as beneficial as any life-process. We find early man overeating to a destructive extent, and, later, carrying his indulgence to heights of refined Epicureanism or depths of gluttony; presently we find religions, one after another, ordering fasts, of days, weeks, even partial fasting for a month, as in the "Ramadan" of the Moslems; or the continued abstinence from certain kinds of food, especially what was most enjoyed; and absurd difficulties and delays in the process, as with the pious Buddhist, "Eating with famished patience, one by one, a thousand grains of millet seed a day."

With this is the underlying objection to all enjoyment, dating back to the pain-economy of primitive savagery, where men practised pain to enable themselves to endure it when it came. That essential error, holding that there is some virtue in pain, is found deep and strong in many religions. Self-denial, renunciation, self-torture even, are so frequently seen in the practice of various religions that they alone would furnish absolute proof of the tremendous power of ideas, however false and foolish.

Consider the asceticism of the early Christians, and see it still in the flagellants of Mexico; think of the revolting tortures borne by the Hindu fakirs; see the ultra-virtuous Greek monk being built into a small cave, with only a hole through which to receive bread and water until he dies, and deny if you can the efficacy of religion to affect conduct.   In the face of nature, against all desires and instincts, some utterly absurd religious idea will produce conduct to make gods laugh or angels weep.

This dominance of religion over behavior is so generally accepted in some lines as to make elaborate proof seem unnecessary; yet it is interesting to trace its influence, not only in these instances of direct opposition to natural law but in the far wider field of required conduct which has no relation to anything.

The most conspicuous feature of any religion is in its rites and ceremonies. We might fill a book with endless lists of such detailed practices, from solemn sacrifice and grand processional to ridiculous minutiæ of costume and diet.

See what religion has done with prayer, for instance.

Prayer, the direct reaching out of the personal consciousness toward the divine force, is obscured, in one religion after another, with all manner of petty directions. We are instructed to pray at certain hours, as if God was to be reached only by appointment; in certain postures, as if the soul could move freely only when the body was on its knees; facing in a given direction, taking off the shoes, holding the hands thus and so, and using various set forms of speech. In the Christian churches God is still addressed in "King James's English." "O Thou!" we say, when we should consider it undignified and foolish to begin, "O You!" and "Thou knowest," rather than the tedious colloquialism, "You know!"

Praying with a string of beads is a widely known method in more than one religion, somewhat as the abacus is used in counting; and in Tibet we find not only beads but the ever-working prayer-mill and the practical but, to our minds, undignified, prayer-spit-ball.

Jesus, used to close contact with the divine spirit, gave clear directions to his followers not to make long prayers in public like the Pharisees, but for each man to go into his closet and pray alone. Yet in our highly elaborated Christian religion a regular ceremony in church, and in other meetings, is precisely that forbidden by Jesus—the making of long prayers in public.

Selected days and seasons for special religious ceremonies, some wholly arbitrary, some mere survivals of ancient customs, are another instance. We have a particularly amusing case in point in our patching together of Sunday and the fourth commandment.

The Sabbath day, to be kept holy, was distinctly described as the seventh day of the week, following upon six days of our labor as it did upon six days of God's labor in making the earth. This day was so kept and is still kept without break by the Hebrews, to whom the direction belongs. Jesus, it will be recalled, paid small attention to it. The Christian church in its mistaken attempt to connect the two religions, adopted the commandments, but selected another day to keep holy. That it should choose the first day of the week instead of the seventh, and use this day in commemoration of the resurrection of Jesus, is as reasonable as any other choice, but that it should advance a commandment applying to another day, commemorating another

event, to buttress its selection, is not so reasonable.   Nothing but minds whose reasoning processes had been paralyzed for ages could build
religious ceremonies and civil laws about a certain day, and quote as authority directions clearly
applying to another one.

The law of inertia seems to work in mental
action as in physical; an idea once started goes
on until something stops it; an idea, stationary,
remains so until something starts it.   In the affairs of practical life our ideas and theories
are constantly started by new events and conditions, and as constantly brought to a standstill
by running up against the facts.   In the field of
religious requirement facts were ignored; or in
specific rites and ceremonies there were none to be
considered.

The body of minute directions developed by
the priest tribe of the Hebrews, had a foundation in sanitary care of food and of the body,
but it soon outstepped the domain of knowledge
and ran riot in absurd detail, such as forbidding
garments of linen and woolen mixed (think of
the "linsey-woolsey" of our pious ancestors!)
and the dismissal as "abominations" of all

clams, oysters, scallops, crabs, and lobsters. This is very clear and sweeping, Leviticus xi, 10:

> And all that have not fins and scales in the seas, and in the rivers, of all that move in the waters, and of any living thing which is in the waters, they shall be an abomination unto you.

Real ethical value must rest on proven consequences, but it is easily possible to attribute virtue, or sin, to the most petty and inconsequential of actions. So we find that religion in its effect upon human conduct, while it has worked great service in many lines, has in some cases urged conduct of an unnatural and undesirable character, and in others has resulted in a vast body of artificial requirements which have served only to confuse and delay our ethical advance.

Every great religious teacher has rebelled against the gathered crust of irrelevant habit, and taught new truth, none more sincerely and powerfully than Jesus; but always the church, though founded on the new truth, has gone on under the influence of the law of inertia, developing a complicated mass of practices quite unrelated to that truth.

In view of the supreme importance of religion
as our chief director in conduct, it is especially
to be regretted that so much of its force has been
spent in trifling performances similar to the petty
ritual of courts, or to some complicated game.
Children delight to set up arbitrary restrictions
for themselves, as in going to school without
stepping on a crack, or without touching wood.
So the childhood of the race has hindered its
own progress with similar idle commands.

But we have not yet reached the most general,
far-reaching, and disastrous of these effects.
Whatever were the doctrines held, the one universal requirement of all religions was belief.
Whatever the laws laid down, always the universal requirement was obedience.   To believe
and to obey—these were the chief demands of religion upon the human mind.   Moreover, this
belief and this obedience were always given to
the Past.

A religion is the strongest cultural influence
affecting humanity.   One and all, religions have
their original prophets, their sacred books, their
traditions of ages gone.   One and all require us

to accept without question what other people long dead have said or written; to obey without question the commands of those behind us. In some cases a religion is held to be the direct work of God, in others merely that of a great teacher, but always they date from far in the past.

Now look at social progress and see what religion has done to it.

Life is endlessly progressive. It develops under pressure of that third great law, Improvement—Evolution. Its beginnings were small indeed; its way lay upward. We ourselves, starting from the status of the human animal, had all our work before us in developing humanity. In that development, even such as we have made, every forward step involves doing something which was not done before. Every step upward is a new one. We may take wrong steps, to be sure, but unless we move, unless we leave the past and go on, there is no progress.

Think, then, of an influence which has tried by every method of a highly cultivated psychology to nail us down, to hold us always subject to the ideas and theories of our remote and ignorant progenitors! What "the fathers" saw and thought was the best they could see and think, no doubt, but to force their limitations on an ever-growing race was a crucial mistake.   No matter what the belief, if it had modestly said, "This is our best thought, go on, think farther!" then we could have smoothly outgrown our early errors and long since have developed a religion such as would have kept pace with an advancing world.   But we were made to believe and not allowed to think.   We were told to obey, rather than to experiment and investigate.   We were always set with our faces toward the remote past, and filled with tales of the great and good and noble men of those old days.

With this tremendous influence so dragging at our heels, it is not surprising to find our irresistible social development more marked in every other department of life than those most affected by religion.   Even in these other lines religion has tried to hinder.   Each new discovery in science was long opposed by religion.   Faith, obedience, and past-worship do not give us new inventions, nor tend to alter conditions we find hard.

The mind is the field of social progress.   Such

mental development as shall enable us to see clearly, to judge wisely, and to govern our conduct according to such judgment, is required for that progress. Yet this strongest of all forces wherewith to improve conduct has widely failed because religion has denied the possibility of such improvement.

See Buddha misleading countless millions by that initial mistake of calling existence evil because it is subject to change and decay. It is very limited thinking which can look upon death and not see it as merely an essential step in life. For the individual it may seem an evil, but for the race it is as unnoticeable as is the death, in a living body, of daily millions of its innumerable constituent cells.

See the ancient Hebrews calling work a curse —work, which is our distinctive social function, in and through which we grow.

See the Brahmans perpetuating a hideous caste system by their sacred books. "Never shall the king flay a Brahman, though convicted of all possible crimes; let him banish the offender from his realm, but with all his property secure and his body unhurt."

See our own faith handicapping Christianity by linking it with Judaism. And overlaying its splendid active teaching of God in man, of worship in human love and service, with a labored theory of salvation the only basis of which is damnation—damnation for that Original Sin of the Babylonian legend, a mythical Adam eating a mystical apple.

Newton drew great thoughts from the fall of an apple, but how much more potent, how incredibly disastrous is that prodigious fruit one little bite from which was enough to warrant a just God in the eternal damnation of the human race! Could there be given a better single proof of the restrictive influence of a religion than this: to require thinking beings to believe such a story, and to use it as a fitting base for the whole pitiful "scheme of salvation"!

Marvelous indeed is it to see the lifting power of truth forcing its upward way through ancient dogmas. Mankind is better than its religions, and as it grew in spite of all obstacles it has lifted religion to its present stage, where man may think without being therefore excommunicated. In each lasting faith there is some truth.

That truth has lived and grown.   One after another, various religions have taught us, some more, some less.   No one can fail to see the uplifting influence of Mohammedanism upon the tribes of northern Africa, the wise beneficence of Confucianism, the gentle unselfishness of Buddhism, the softening, strengthening power of Christianity.   There is no higher light, no greater help, to guide our steps, than religion, if that religion rests on natural law.

That is precisely why it is of such vital importance that a religion should see truth as something growing, something to be continually sought and followed bravely to the dawn of better days on earth; and precisely why such immeasurable harm has been done by the static quality of our previous ones.   In all ways they affect our conduct more forcibly than any other influence, sometimes for good, sometimes for evil, sometimes for mere delay.

If we look at the great stationary religions of Asia, we see a high development of intellect but a low development of life.   Progress, in our sense of improved living conditions, the Orientals do not desire.   Life being an evil to be escaped, why indeed should any one waste time trying to make it a little easier? These peoples remain static. They preserve the most ancient customs, do not ask for nor seek anything better than was sustained by their ancestors. The man, proprietor of the woman, makes all the rules which govern her life. He desires a son, for religious reasons, but has small interest in daughters, save to see them married, that they may give some other man a son.

If we accept the postulate that our main duty here is to improve the human race and the world it makes, then all these static religions are to be condemned in so far as they do not tend to improvement. But if our main postulate is that life here is only a necessary evil, a mere stepping stone to life elsewhere, then there is indeed no reason for taking thought for the morrow on earth.

Since such is the main postulate of all the death-based religions, and since those religions are largely responsible for present conditions, we must look more carefully into this main feature of masculine dominance in religious thought.

CHAPTER XI

THE NATURAL BEGINNING OF AN UNNATURAL RELATION

IN order to form a fair judgment of the effect of a too-masculine influence upon religion we must have a definite idea of normal human development. This is a stage of life quite beyond the mere maintenance of the species. The human animal is the constituent base of humanity, but humanity itself is a relationship of these animals, in course of which they develop qualities we call "human." These are without exception collective, inter-relative.

The human animal may exist, has existed, for thousands of years, with hardly any progress in this relationship; it may develop a degree of humanness, and thereafter become decadent, less human. It may reach a high degree of humanness, and remain stationary. It may continually develop, with no necessary limit to be seen. Hu-

manity is an organic relationship, open to un-
limited development, into which the human
animal has entered with varying success. Our
history is, or would be if it were based on genu-
ine social knowledge, a record of experiments
in humanness, most of which, to date, have
failed.

If we take the earliest stage of savage life
known to us, and compare it with the best advantages of civilization, we have the line of direction of social progress. If we analyze those
advantages and the essential steps in their for-
mation, we know the way in which we have
become human.

The primary necessity is, of course, advantage to the individual animal. If society did not
keep its constituents alive and promote their happiness and reproductiveness, there would be no
society. Yet with this preliminary benefit to individuals there follows a surrender of personal
liberty, a modification to social advantage which
quite often involves individual loss. This is
most easily seen in the earliest forms of association, as where low tribal groups share their food
in time of need; and in the progressive heroism

developed in group fighting, to the heights of "dying for our country."

But far beyond the advantage to its individual constituents, a society, if progressing freely, develops structural and functional characters which have no immediate connection with individual survival. Such a social function as road-making we can see to be of advantage to the builders, as to thousands of others, but such a social functionary as a poet is not so easily explained. Being a poet is seldom very profitable to that person. He might thrive better as a banker or a broker or even a burglar. Group service is not always of personal advantage.

In social economics the basic function is excess production by some parts and distribution of product to parts otherwise employed. The released energy of the other parts expresses itself in development of further functions. Social progress consists in and rises by such functional development; in the manufacture of those varied mechanical products which are the means of present advantage and further development; in the evolution of industrial and other arts, of education, science, and religion. A normal social development, therefore, would show us groups of increasing size and complexity, in which all individuals were functioning for the social advantage, with widening power and pleasure, and were themselves provided for in a far higher and surer condition of health and happiness than would have been possible to them as detached, self-serving persons.

The first necessity of an organic form is to distribute nourishment from mouth to stomach to its uttermost members, members the use of which is increasingly valuable, but which cannot feed themselves. Our system of payment is the social return to the individual for his work, but that work is always for other people. The more highly specialized we become as social servants, the less able we are to "take care of ourselves."

The extreme subtlety and unmeasured advantages of our social organic life with the social consciousness and all its instincts of mutual love and service, should long since have brought us to a condition of unparalleled prosperity and happiness, and yet when we compare the human race with lower species we find many disadvantageous features in our kind, quite beyond those common to other creatures.

Other animals have parasites; so have we. Other animals are subject to disease and death; so are we. Other animals have their enemies and competitors; so have we. Other animals have to face difficulties and hardships and exert themselves to secure food; so do we. But with all these common conditions no other animal is so frequently sick and defective, so given to various deformities, especially in the mind, so persistent in self-injuring behavior.

A certain balance between the creature and its environment is observed in other species. The spirit of the animal fits the body, the body expresses the spirit; each living thing is so adapted to its conditions that it can do what it wishes and wishes to do what it can.

Adaptation to the environment is a safe definition of natural happiness. Any creature not so adapted is unhappy, necessarily; and, since conditions change, that creature is happiest which can most readily adapt itself to a changed environment. Beyond this lies the still higher capacity for modifying the environment to suit the needs of the creature. If the food supply stops in winter, then one animal hibernates like the bear, others migrate like the birds, while another modifies the environment to suit its needs by storing food, like the squirrel or the beaver. Many construct shelter, for themselves and their young, and some even change their clothes with the season, wearing a thinner coat in summer, a thicker one in winter; sometimes carefully matching their winter clothing to the snow, for business reasons.

Man not only is the most adaptable of species, found in all climates, on all soils, eating all foods, but he has by far the greatest capacity for modifying the environment to suit his needs. By the use of clothing, fire, and shelter, he can make a little climate of his own in the arctic regions; or with fan, parasol, and noonday siesta, survive in the tropics.

The advantages of the human species over every other are so marked, so enormous, that our miseries are all the more ridiculous and discreditable. With the power of making life easier, richer, smoother, better, more swiftly progressive, we see humanity so overwhelmed with difficulty and suffering that we have called this lovely world "a vale of tears."

Among our peculiar distresses the mind of man has struggled in perplexity and dismay. Able to visualize, to generalize, to form abstractions, he soon postulated what he called "the problem of evil," and has striven to solve that problem by all manner of arbitrary explanations.

We cannot blame primitive man for being unable to grasp the evolutionary philosophy, nor his later descendants for not seeing beyond the knowledge of their time. But we can inquire what sort of initial mistake it was which in this species has led to such lamentable results.

The essential distinctions of the human race are all advantages. That handle of all tools, the human hand; that maker of all tools, the human brain—these alone set us far above all other creatures. Our irrepressible growth in skill and knowledge, the development of capacity for organization, for profound research, for exquisite inter-service, with the ascending delight which

accompanies the fulfilment of high function—
these should make humanity the happiest thing
alive.

Yet natural social development is continually arrested and distorted by our own behavior.
To what peculiarity may we look for an apparently innate perversity so universal as to give
rise to all manner of devil-myths and ghastly
gods of torment?

The major position taken in this book—that
religion, our greatest help in conscious progress,
has been injured by coming through the minds of
men alone—leads to the natural question of why
the male of our species should so be blamed while
the males of other species are harmless and
useful.

Here we reach the biological basis for that
"innate perversity," for the peculiar behavior of
the species which has so opposed and retarded
its natural progress.   This lies, not in any essential fault in the male of our race, but in his unnatural relation to the female.   By the early and
universal subjection of the female to the male,
by her segregation to the lowest form of service
and to an exaggerated sex-development, we have

made ourselves a crippled race, a race whose whole development was left to be carried on by one half of it.

It is the strange, lonely, unnatural position of the human male, accentuated beyond all reason by his cumulative over-development in sex, which quite easily accounts for that "perversity." It is not the natural male in a natural relation who works evil, to religion or anything else, but our human speciality, the male of the species carrying on all the social activities as best he can, while served and catered to by the other half of the race.

That these conditions have begun to change is the most hopeful fact in our present life, but it will be many generations before we can show the equally human pair capable of carrying on the smooth and happy development of society. In hastening so desirable a movement it is more than necessary for us to understand the precise nature of the previous morbid condition, with its un- avoidable evil results.

The bitterness and antagonism aroused by the recent struggle of women to reach normal human development, was enhanced by their not unnatu-

ral blame of men for their unjust treatment.
"Tyrant man" was treated as an opponent, condemned and berated for his cruelty. Such a
position was well warranted at the time, but
it has no bearing on the initial problem of how
this great misplacement started.

Just as early religions were animistic, and natural objects and forces personified, so women
sought to explain the new charge of "original
sin" by assuming a man with a club who suddenly rose up against his female and subjugated
her by main force. Being ignorant of biological
processes they did not realize how absurd it was
to imagine a relation as old as sex itself to have
been instantaneously changed and inverted by
one man—or one generation of men.

The freedom and power of the female were unbroken after the male appeared, up to and well
into the human race. In the earliest known
stages of our savage state the female was still
free, useful, and honored. Between that time and
the beginnings of history, a period of enormous
length, the change took place. It appears to
have occurred at about the same stage of primitive culture, in widely separated races, in various

parts of the earth. Reasons for such a change must be looked for in the race itself; it must be due to some inherent distinction peculiar to the human animal, and manifesting itself at a certain stage of development.

Such inherent distinction is not far to seek.

The human race is characterized by the prolongation of infancy, this prolongation increasing with human development.

The prolongation of infancy involved an extension of motherhood; not only in length, as the period of infancy grew longer, but in breadth, as the mother was called upon to serve more than one child at the same time, of different ages, having different wants.

The extension of motherhood, in the human animal, with its skilful hand, its thinking brain, manifested itself not only in the nurture and defense given by lower mothers but in the beginnings of industry. Within their limits we see the same force working in lower creatures. All the endless labor and care, all the complex organization and varied products of the bees and ants and other insects are the efforts of motherhood. Motherhood is the great developer, throughout nature. With us it poured out its rising flood of love in service, in work, in the making of things, in the securing, storing, and preparing of food. Note this last.

The mother was the first worker. Her mate was still only a hunter and fighter. The initial steps in all the primitive industries were taken by women alone.

Work is a human distinction; the human distinction par excellence. Through work alone have we developed our special race capacities. The female as the race type naturally developed along racial lines. The fact that her labors were for the child gives them no character of sex. As was earlier shown, the variation in the reproductive process is a race distinction, manifested before sex was introduced. This prolongation of infancy was a race-improvement, and its attendant development of mother-power was also a race distinction, having no bearing upon the natural sex relation. Nevertheless it is precisely her increased capacity for human service which lies at the root of our great race tragedy, the subjugation of the female. This came about not by any act of cruelty on the part of man but by the increasing desirability of woman's services.

In all other races the female is desirable to the male merely as a female; she has no further value to him.   In our race, by the industrial development of woman, the female assumed a new attraction, not that of sex, but that of service. As she increased in usefulness, as her children grew older and larger, yet still profited by her intelligent care, as she learned to prepare food for them, why should not he partake of it?   He was not much older than his oldest son, for primitive life was short; her motherliness to this day extends to her husband; it so extended then.   Of course he liked it; he does yet.   Easily and unconsciously he slipped into more and more dependence on her services.   She was of economic value to him, as is no other female to a male. It is motherhood of which he first took advantage, not sex.   In some low cultures we still find women slaves in economics but free and respected in sex.

There is a distinction between industry, in all its wide specialization,—with the resultant distribution and exchange of products which form the economic base of social life,—and service, which is a personal relation. Personal service is necessary to infancy; it is normal and right. Personal service of the female to the adult male is abnormal and wrong. It is no more right that a healthy man should be waited on like a baby by a woman than that a healthy woman should be fed and clothed by a man.

This grown baby, enjoying a mother's care and service long after it was normal, grew to depend on it. There must have been some advantage in the absurd relation, in those dark old days, to account for its wide development. Obviously a fighting male, served and mothered by a working female, was a more competent warrior than one who had to stop fighting and take care of himself. The Mexican soldiery still take their women with them to wait on them.

The economic value of the female is quite sufficient to account for an increasing demand for her possession; the more women a man had to work for him, the more rich and comfortable he was. But extensive polygamy and the sex slavery resultant could not appear until cattle-keeping and, in time, a settled agriculture gave at last the house, and the house-keeper. It is the economic value of the woman which makes men so sure that "A woman's place is the home."

Our persistent misunderstanding in the matter is due to our general confusion of sex and service. Yet it is clear to any fair observer that the woman whose place is in the home is first of all the serving mother (the man never ceases to dwell lovingly on her service); and after that, may be, the wife, the sister, the daughter, the aunt—any sort of female relative who does not have to be paid—or, at worst, a "hired girl." The main idea is that the man must be served by women.

Sex attraction has no bearing at all on domestic service, unless as a matter of propinquity. The domestic virtues we so extol are useful where they are needed, in the private home, but the women who command the widest sex admiration are frequently in the most public and undomestic positions, as performers in a circus, theater, or music-hall. Our *jeunesse dorée* marry chorus girls more frequently than parlor-maids.

But the continuous service of the primitive woman to her mate soon became an immovable race custom, settling into sharply marked distinctions between "man's work" and "woman's work," ancient taboos which we are only now outgrowing.   With the advantage of the woman's services increasing as race faculties developed, they became more and more desirable, and the willing work of the mother slowly sank into slavery.   Slave women were visibly of more use than slave men.   The women could do more things, were not so combative, were soon sex slaves as well as economic ones, and added to their value the supreme gift of motherhood.   They being his, their children were his, and the sons of slave mothers were more easily compelled to service than the free man captured in battle.

So we find the simple, natural, unavoidable extension of motherhood into service, taken advantage of by the adult male by slow degrees, becoming a settled custom, and inevitably developing into slavery.

In following out the results of such extension, we must first note the immense difference between the survival and development of humanity, which is a progressive form of social relationship, and the mere persistence of the human animal.

The reason our species can go wrong more widely than any other and not die of it, is because of our social economic functions. While we lived by hunting and fishing, our existence was precarious, our progress slow, and any marked error in behavior met the same prompt death sentence so clearly seen in lower races. Even the pastoral tribes were limited by almost similar economic restrictions. If the grass failed, or the cattle failed, they failed too.

But when agriculture was reached, man conquerered his food supply; and that by the exertion of only a portion of his powers. The labor of some could now feed others, an increasing proportion of others as the processes of cultivation of food improved.

Given a basis of physical existence like this, and given women sufficiently well treated to produce more people, the persistence of the human species was secured. But no more. Social progress was now possible, but not by any means assured. We find in Africa low cultures based on agriculture, with woman-slavery, which have apparently stayed at that level for uncounted ages.

Where progress did appear, it was open to any amount of error which did not cut off the source of supply, motherhood plus agriculture. This primal source has kept the human race alive on earth through ages of unnecessary evils which would have long since extinguished any other species. One early tribe has given way to another; one far higher people has been destroyed by another; and one culture after another has died of self-made diseases and follies, but the race survives and has developed in various places and distributed far and wide those inventions and discoveries, arts and sciences which make us harder to kill than early man.

Before any religion worthy of the name was developed we find the race already established on the basis of woman-slavery, and, later, its inevitable consequence—man-slavery as well. Our culture, for all historic time up to a few centuries ago, was a slave culture, we in America, to our shame, being the last civilized people to abolish this primitive evil.

The male, master of the female, carrying on his mastership to other men, developing industry by force, as a tribute, a degradation, brought his prejudices to bear on every early religion in its formative period, and kept them in action through all later years.

We who have passed it, can now see the essential evils of slavery. It acts upon the slave, with well-known weakening results. It acts upon the master, tending to produce pride, laziness, and self-indulgence, cruelty, injustice, and, from its dim beginnings to its glaring end, licentiousness. Where the slave was of a different race and color, this last result was evidenced beyond any possible dispute.

When characteristics like these have formed the minds of men for ages, the influence of those minds upon religion is sadly evident. Facing the evils in behavior inevitably developed by his position as master, man vainly sought, by stern commandments, to prohibit the behavior, while maintaining the cause. The master himself becoming, through long slaveholding, proud, lazy, selfish, cruel, and unjust, it is no wonder that his early gods were all of these together.

The habit of mastership, growing as improved conditions made larger the group of subject workers, stretched out and on, unchecked by any truer concept of social life, and gave us kings. The son of a slave was a slave, the son of a master was a master. Here is the philosophic base for "the divine right of kings," and all those pursuant customs of inheritance and primogeniture, the forcing of a trade from father to son, and a number of like collateral errors.

In the case of lower animals, it is true we must look to birth as the only line of development in a race. But social evolution is not a physical process. The variations of human genius are not confined to family lines; the gifts which make us great come not through the children of Phidias and Aristotle, of Shakspere and Edison, but through their works.

In a normal social evolution we should have seen the gradual differentiation of our varied gifts, the products of our varied abilities, the distribution of those products so as best to promote social progress, and the careful cultivation of all children so as to secure the maximum of social efficiency. A normal development of religion meanwhile, seeing the broad road of progress as the line to be followed in right doing, would have strengthened our joy in good workmanship, exhorted us to mutual appreciation and inter-service, kept before us the splendid hope of race-improvement.

But man, master of women and of slaves, had quite other habits of mind.   Recognizing clearly enough the deadly results of iniquity, he summoned, to account for his behavior, theories of fate and the devil; and to prevent wrong-doing, used the only power he knew—command—with threat of punishment and promise of reward.

Our man-modified religions have never recognized the basic evils of subject womanhood, and its resultant, slavery.   Within a lifetime we heard the preachers of our South—yes, and many in the North as well—defending slavery on the ground that Jesus had not objected to it, and that St. Paul told Onesimus to obey his master. Yet they might have found one text, Exodus xxi, 16, which certainly had an adverse bearing on the slave-trade:

And he that stealeth a man, and selleth him, or if he be found in his hand, he shall surely be put to death.

As to the subjection of woman, the key to the whole position, none of the old religions objected to that as wrong. On the contrary, they one and all assumed her to be the natural inferior of man and to be endured only for his use and convenience, because, forsooth, it was "not good that the man should be alone." In view of what we now know as to his relative origin, this becomes charmingly funny.

The man's mind influenced the religion, and the religion, petrified and immovable, influenced the man's mind, and so, inevitably, the woman's. Because of its heavy injunctions as to the woman's duty of submission to him, that submission has been enforced long after changed conditions would have led to freedom.

We can see in actual fact women working with men in many peasantries, and even in domestic industry, showing racial abilities, with some approach to recognition. Wherever freedom of choice was allowed, they manifested human capacities in several trades. As life moved on, changing and broadening, so would women have grown had they been free. But religion did not move, change, grow. Religion was supposed to be final, to be "the truth," all the truth there was.

Our belief in salvation rests on a previous damnation; damnation rests on "original sin," —the eating of forbidden fruit,—and that requires belief in the story of Eden. If the ancient Hebrew religion accepted the still more ancient Assyrian legend, stating that woman was made out of Adam's rib, for his personal accommodation, and that her subsequent interest in apples was responsible for the loss of that horticultural paradise, it is not remarkable that the pious modern Hebrew still mutters his daily prayer of masculine superiority, thanking God that he was not born a woman.

One religion after another has accepted and perpetuated man's original mistake in making a private servant of the mother of the race.

CHAPTER XII

IN the brief outline given in Chapter III something was indicated of the profound effect of the death-interest of early man, the fighter; and of the further results of this prepossession upon our later religious thought.

The beneficent processes of natural growth go on so unconsciously that it was long before we were led to speculate upon them, while the painful and injurious processes of our misbehavior were so prominent, so unpleasantly forced upon our consciousness that our early meditations were centered on them perforce.

The patent miseries of women were so heartbreakingly evident that some story of a deserved punishment had to be evolved to account for them. The black shame and grief of slavery also required a reason, and divine sanction was again arranged to justify it. The general suffering and uncertainty of human life during the period when fighting was still the most honored profession, also called for explanation, and was met with various theories.

Natural death is not so frequent, so terrible, even so undesired a thing, as to call for justification; but the torrent of destruction brought upon humanity by the continuous warfare of the dominant male, maintained all our miseries at the hightest pitch, and similarly maintained our speculations upon them. Again and again some favorably placed people has developed in peace long enough to produce great works, and lay the foundations of further civilization, and again and again some fresh flood of hungry fighting males from another country has overwhelmed and destroyed them. The latest and worst outbreak of this primitive horror in modern history is seen in the German overflow of greed and destruction.

The long persistence through all the ages of this unnecessary killing not only kept sudden death by slaughter continually before us, the death of strong young men, but famine and pestilence, inevitable consequences of warfare, destroyed women and children spared by the sword.

As if this were not enough death, the excessive indulgence of the dominant male supplied us with a special set of diseases of peculiarly unpleasant effects, and distributed them as far as men went either in warfare or commerce; while such contagion as they gathered abroad was brought home and distributed among wives and children.

Social progress must indeed have had behind it the rising force of evolution to make any headway at all under this régime.   It is no wonder that "human nature" and its works were called evil.   Its reactive effect upon the minds of men and so upon their religion is the result we are here observing.

Man's life being obviously so bad, so foolishly bad and painful, his mind, seeking explanation, speculated without end upon "the origin of evil."   Having the minds of men only, heavily overmasculized by long surrender to impulses originally natural, some of these early thinkers inevitably staged the universe as a conflict.   In the Zoroastrian view we have two initial principles assumed, of Good and Evil; in cruder philosophies we set up conflicting persons, god and the devil.   Never did these profound thinkers admit that the trouble was of their own making, and could be stopped when they chose.

A strange, irresponsible weakness of mind is shown; a failure to connect in the relation between behavior and consequence; a willingness to blame something, anything, except ourselves, and to seek some recompense for suffering in any kind of future life, rather than to stop it here. It is this effect upon our minds and through them upon religion; this separation of religion from conduct which has maintained so long the infant errors of the human race.   Our bad behavior is like that of some moron, lacking in moral sense and incapable of self-control.   If such mental deficiency can be shown as due to bone pressure on the brain, and that pressure be removed, an immediate improvement in conduct may be looked for.

It is not enough to explain the perturbed course of human development as an initial mistake, such as we have shown in the subjugation of women;

for the course of social evolution would have led to the outgrowing of that evil—as, indeed, it is now doing.

The pressure which has prevented our mental development along lines of ethical improvement is the pressure of wrong ideas. Even in the open ground of industrial and mechanical advance it is slow work to move the reluctant brain aside from the lines of habit; but when to natural impulse we add a morbid development, to that the customs and laws of centuries, and to that the sanction of religion, it is no wonder that our behavior improves so slowly.

The strange lack of connection between our accumulating knowledge and our persistent foolishness, which allows us to believe for ages in a religion teaching chastity and love, while going on in unchastity and warfare just the same, must be accounted for. Deep-seated and unceasingly powerful, as a cause of this disconnection, is man's primary diversion of religion from life.

When we know more of practical psychology, understanding the weighty influence of the inside world we make by thinking, or have made for us and inserted in our minds by other people's thinking, it will be easier to see and appreciate that vast artificial structure of the mind, a religion. We are beginning to hear much of "a complex," mainly in certain specific lines; it is only the name which is new. We used to call it "a state of mind," which is an even better term.

If a person admits to his mind such and such beliefs, he gets his mind into a "state" under which it reacts in a manner suitable to those beliefs. A religion, starting with certain assumptions, goes on from good to better or from bad to worse, inevitably. This is equally true with any group of ideas, but in most cases the state of mind is brought into contact with a group of facts, and facts are stubborn things.

The peculiarity of all death-based religions is that their subject-matter is entirely outside of facts. Men could think and think, talk and argue, advance, deny, assert, and controvert, and write innumerable books, without being hampered at any time by any fact. The nearest they came to such foundation was in seeking to establish some facts as to the lives of their various religious teachers, or the identity of their sacred

books; and even here there is far more of myth
and legend than any certainty.

Thus we have almost from the beginning the
assertion of authority which it was impossible to
disprove, a sin to doubt, an indiscretion even
to consider.   Then, with this arbitrary basis, the
minds of men soared happily in unbridled con-
jecture, and built up colossal systems of thought,
racial "complexes" or states of mind, which were
imposed upon the world.   Each ancient religion
has its form of established church, its priesthood
or clergy, its temples and system of ceremonies;
and each, as a social phenomenon, stands in history as a social complex, "a state of mind," a
system of ceremonies, rather than as an agent
of improvement.

Each religion has made some improvement.
Each has had some truth in its basic assumption, some result in human conduct; else
they could not have endured; but its essential
limitations make each immovable religion less
and less useful in a moving world.

To-day, in our own faith, we see more freedom and swifter change than used to be possible
in many centuries.   In a church which insists

on infallible authority we naturally find less general education, less freedom of thought, and greater emphasis on maintaining the proper state of mind. The religious ceremonies of such a church are predominantly emotional, and the required conduct largely consists in petty rites.

Another, balancing carefully among the moving facts of life, knowing too much to believe literally as our remote predecessors believed, yet unwilling to admit any error in its creeds, has developed a loose elasticity of thought which may "interpret" anything to mean anything else, as it pleases.   It recites creeds which it does not believe, yet thinks it wrong to change.   Why? Creeds, surely, are not "inspired."

Everywhere among progressive peoples religion is waking up, is seeing the need of fuller expression in living, is extending its demands from mere personal performances to newly perceived social duties.   But against the rising force of natural progress still stands the huge dead weight of the old race complex, that artificially induced and maintained "state of mind" the major theme of which is always death.

We see even to-day the movement of those

quaint reactionaries called "Fundamentalists," who advance as the "fundamentals" of the Christian religion the group of miracles and legends surrounding the origin and death of Jesus, laying no emphasis whatever on what it was he taught. Here is the persistence of the death-based theoretical "faith" as apart from a system of living. Its main appeal is for belief, that the believer may so be "saved" in the "other life." The evangelist still uses this appeal. So widely popular a revivalist as Billy Sunday holds up the same promise of heaven or threat of hell—mostly the latter—as was effective among the illiterate and the heathen two thousand years ago.

The early Christians themselves firmly believed in the imminent destruction of the world and their prompt personal reward for martyrdom. St. Paul is perfectly clear about this. He saw no use in being brave without payment.

If after the manner of men I have fought with beasts at Ephesus, what advantageth it me, if the dead rise not? let us eat and drink; for to morrow we die.

There is, of course, much in the slow, irregular rise of religious application to life which is due only to our racial limitations, and cannot be attributed to the influence of sex.   But we can still see the marked checks and perversions which are clearly due to that one cause; to the monopolization of religious thought and doctrines and the establishment of creeds by men alone.

A doctrine as to a future life has small application to this one.   A creed may be learned, believed, recited, and defended valiantly as a cherished possession—"Hold ye the faith, the faith our fathers sealed us!"—without its having any prominent effect upon life.   The future hopes or fears of Moslem, Jew, or Christian do not differentiate their habits in warfare or in business to any appreciable extent.

We may show the specific results of an exclusively male point of view in many fields of life, but in none more importantly than in rigid devotion to arbitrary "faiths."   In ethics the male influence is plainly shown, perhaps most notably in the before-noted specific exclusion from ethical checks of the special fields of masculine expression, "All's fair in love and war."

In economics we see the enormous evils still visible from the institution of slavery and its resultant false views of labor.   In the sex relation itself the evil wrought is evident to any student; as is the further mischief of degrading the character of women and retarding normal race-improvement.   But under and over and beyond all these is the wholesale crippling of the human mind, by insisting on unreasoning belief in early misconceptions and forbidding the use of reason in the most important field of our conscious life —the development and application of higher forms of religion.

It cannot be too strongly asserted that the insistence on blind, unreasoning faith is due mainly to the maintenance of a subject-matter upon which there was no knowledge, namely the "other world"; and that this basis was assumed because of early man's preoccupation with death. It is, unfortunately, quite possible to believe a thing which is contradicted by facts, especially if the facts are not generally known; but if the whole position on which we rested our religions had been visibly opposed by what we did know, even the unthinking masses would, in time have noticed it.

For instance, if we were told that a bad man

could never grow rich, it would overtax our most willing faith to believe it. But when we are told that it is difficult, well-nigh impossible for a rich man to get into heaven, we can believe that easily, especially if we are poor men; there is no evidence against it.

The soaring, imaginative minds of men, constructing lofty, shimmering piles of abstract thought, and taking as their postulate a revelation from God, gave us religions which could not possibly be maintained without belief and obedience: all early religions demand these. In proportion as they are given, the religions endure, and we find them most permanent and changeless among peoples who make the least effort to square their beliefs with the laws of life.

It is not mere ignorance which holds down a religion. The wisdom of each age was largely developed by the priests. But this wisdom was never applied to their basic doctrines; these were immovable. It was not lack of capacity for thought which maintained absurdities and contradictions. The Hindu mind is perhaps more highly developed in concentrated, abstract thought than that of any other race, but the

Hindu's limitless range of meditation and deduction all starts from certain assumed premises, unprovable premises, "irrelevant, incompetent, and immaterial" premises, and we see that tremendous mental exercise resulting in a race of a few sublimely intellectual and useless devotees and preachers, with millions of pathetically ignorant and unprogressive believers.

Intellectual activity is naturally evolved as a means to modify conduct, for the advantage of its possessor; the animal's intelligence for service of self and young, that of humanity for service of the race. We may wisely use physical gymnastics and athletics in order to develop balanced strength and accuracy for use in living. But the highly specialized acrobat acquires astonishing ability to do things which are of no possible service. He makes a spectacle of himself which we are willing to pay to see, as an amusement. So intellectual gymnastics may be wisely practised in order to develop strength and accuracy of thought for use in living; but while the mental Strong Man and acrobat may be immensely proud of himself, he is of no use to others even as a spectacle.

The original basing of religion upon extra-mundane assumption, and the ensuant erection of immense complicated systems of theology and intricate rules for wholly irrelevant conduct, have had a widely injurious effect in their influence upon education.

In normal mental action, consistency, connection between ideas, is required.   The major distinction of our human mind is in the ability to see connections, to put two and two together. As reasoning beings we are revolted by an illogical absurdity.   But if the oldest, strongest, most universal cultural influence for all mankind is based on unprovable assumptions, involves gross inconsistencies, yet is enforced by all authority, then we deliberately cultivate in the race an artificial capacity for unreasonableness.

Our unreasonableness has been carried on still farther through systems of education.   At first the social function of education was wholly in the hands of the priesthood.   The teacher as such appeared later, and his work was largely the teaching of religion, as is still seen where little Moslems are taught the Koran, little Hindus taught from their sacred books, little Hebrews from theirs; and in our own public schools we still sought to impart something of our religion until our Hebrew and Romanist citizens objected.

The direct teaching of religion is small part of the effect in question. More serious is the acquired ability to dissociate ideas instead of connecting them. To this influence is traceable our adoption of an arbitrary division of studies, the mind of the scholar jerked from one subject to another at the stroke of the clock, without the faintest connection in thought. By such means we train learned men, profoundly informed in certain lines, totally uninformed in others, and never even feeling the need of any connection between what they know and the life and progress of mankind.

Because for so long the Christian church carried on its services and preserved its sacred books in Latin, with Greek and Hebrew behind that, there is still an "odor of sanctity" about these ancient tongues and because, further in the Renaissance, so many ancient though secular books in Greek and Latin were brought to life, for many years education continued to place most of its emphasis upon knowledge of dead languages.

That educated men, men more learned than others, should often at the same time be less reasonable, argues some strange peculiarity in our methods of mental training. This peculiarity is directly inherited from religion. "Learning" for long consisted solely in reading what was written and trying to remember it. As a matter of fact, students never *learned* anything, but confined themselves strictly to what was known before. We are but now beginning to *learn*, by investigation, by experiment, by the honest effort of free and active minds to add to human knowledge, instead of everlastingly repeating old theories.

Even if all the bases of religion had been correct, the enforcement of blind faith, the prohibition of intelligent inquiry would have had an injurious effect upon the mind. A sincere devotion to truth has quite different results. Truth is an ever-opening vista, a thing to be always followed and never caught.

But each religion assumed that it had "the truth," the whole of it, and that no other knowledge was of any particular value. As the sturdy Moslem said when he ordered the burning of the magnificent library at Alexandria, "If these books agree with the Koran, there is no need of them; if they do not, they are false," and this one highly religious and unintelligent man destroyed the work of ages.

Such a person, with the vast loss involved by his action, might well stand in history against that petty figure of mythology, Pandora.

CHAPTER XIII

NATURAL DEVELOPMENT AND EFFECTS OF HER RELIGION

ONLY recently, and as yet only in the minds of a very few, have we learned to think of human life as a continuous, moving thing. Most of us still see humanity merely as a great many people, and history as a collection of reigns and battles.

When we speak of religion as modified by women, the reader promptly visualizes the women he sees to-day, and feels small confidence in any benefit resultant from their influence. Any general knowledge of the world's literature shows how low an opinion men have had of women, and some men are still outspoken in maintaining the ancient view.

Even those modern protagonists of women whom we call "feminists" find some difficulty in proving equality; much more, superiority, in

women, as we know them. These poor little
slouchy creatures, painting their cheeks and pow-
dering their noses, fluttering before our eyes as
willing exponents of every passing fashion,
adopting male vices, and so unutterably traitor-
ous to the essential glory of their own sex as willingly to forego motherhood in order to share the
barren pleasures of the other—are these the
women from whose influence we are to expect
a higher religion?

Most certainly they are not. But these are not
Women. These are really more worthy of that
absurd title with which men have tried to dis-
credit the progressive women of our times—"the
third sex." If we look again at the original relation, follow again its normal development, we
shall see but too clearly how abnormal, how pathetic, how ridiculous is such sad degradation of
womanhood.

As members of the human race, women should
manifest those powers, interests, and achievements which are the measure of social progress.
As females, their essential purpose is to reproduce and to improve the race. Even as house
servants they still have value if their ministra-

tions maintain in happiness and efficiency a socially useful man.

But one who holds herself "above" house service and is below any other kind; who repudiates motherhood; who is valued only as partner in a fruitless sex relation; and who spends her life, her idle life, in amusing herself—this is not a woman, much less a man, and very far from being a human creature.

Yet this is the product of men's misuse of womanhood. The kind of women we most despise is precisely the kind which has been produced by the desire of the dominant male. His demand for children of his own has maintained enough mothers to keep the race going. His demand for house servants has been met by female relatives, by young women before they married, and by some old or neglected ones.

But for their special pleasure men have produced and maintained this other variety, either in frank professional degradation, or in all the shallow margins of what we call "society"— women to play with.

Nothing but a wholly masculine world could have for so long endured this exquisite monstrosity. A living thing, member of the highest race, capable by human nature of some part in the wide range of social service, and by female nature of the noble function of motherhood; cut off from both, used as a sex convenience, called a "necessity" and then despised and punished for her service—this is the extreme form of the women men have made.

Could there be asked a clearer proof of the abnormality of sex-dominance through the male?

The laws of nature are, fortunately, stronger than all our mistakes.

We can interfere with them, pervert and hinder them, but we cannot prevent their ultimate success. Even while culture after culture fell because of its inner disorders, there has been rising in the race a degree of knowledge, a general intelligence, which has at last recognized the more obvious phases of this evil condition, and we are already started on a new stage of human progress.

The change is deeper, more important, than any mere feminist imagines. It is not the attainment of that first poor purpose, "equality with men." Heaven help the world if women could reach no higher than that! Men, free to do as they would, modifying the species through their usurped power of selection, preferring the pretty and foolish women to the strong and brave, and interbreeding with the lowest races whenever so inclined, have brought us only to our present condition of struggle and distress.

They have, it is true, given us all the achievements which constitute social progress. As the only acting members of society they had to do all that was done for it. In comparison women are far behind, and do indeed need to attain equality. But all these upward steps of men have been accompanied by such a steady downward-dragging force of morbid, misplaced sex that our most advanced peoples are still living under conditions of disease, poverty, crime, and ever-renewed warfare, so painful as to make some deny that there is any real progress.

Yet our progress is great and clear. No competent student of social conditions can deny it. That a man is subject to more diseases than a clam does not show the clam to be the higher form. It is only our high human development which has enabled us to endure the mass of unnecessary evils with which we have cumbered our own path upward. But if women were to-day as able in human activities as men, yet could do no better, the change would give no great prospect of a better religion, or a better race.

To grasp the splendid hope which does underlie this change, we must take a fresh hold on the laws of evolution, physical and social, with the true place of sex in life's development.

Sweeping from our minds every misleading ancient legend, let us see clearly what has been happening on earth; where women come in, their special nature, power, and purpose, and particularly the work of motherhood. We see the long process of physical evolution leading up to the human animal; the stream of life pouring like a river, modified by conditions, struggling where struggle was necessary, changing in sudden mutations from some inner urge, and rising in proportion as it produced new powers.

We see the mother, the race type, manifesting new faculties, transmitting her faculties to her young, and devising more and more efficacious means to promote that great process. We see the father, reaching race equality at length, contributing more and more of service to the young. Finally we come to humanity, and the stage of social evolution. In this we find new powers in action.

In lower forms there is no vehicle of life but the physical body. Whatever progress is attained is shown only in the creature itself, is transmitted only from parent to young. Humanity enters upon a superior and wholly different process of development. Our progress is attained through inter-personal qualities and activities, and embodied in the works of our hands; we make things, and our forward movement is to be measured by the things we make. This gain is transmitted far and wide and down all the ages, quite outside of physical heredity. Our human progress is cumulative, continuous, entered upon by generation after generation, each standing on the attainments of those before, and adding to them.

Humanity is a living form which is virtually "immortal" on earth, and subject to constant improvement.

What constitute the forces promoting human improvement?

The major force is that of evolution itself, the law of growth; to that, with us, is added conscious effort; and to that, again, our supreme function of humaniculture, education, wherein we see a conscious society gathering up its best achievements and so applying them to the young as enormously to facilitate the natural processes of growth.

We do not have to re-discover in slow experiment what our predecessors knew.   That which, with us, cannot be transmitted physically is transmitted socially, through education in its largest sense, including every trade and craft and art and science.

Thus we see in humanity a form of life collective, organic, as natural as any others, as open to unconscious progress as those behind it, but richer far in power of action, able to recognize and promote its own evolution.   If we can imagine some orohippus or pliohippus, some intermediate form between the eohippus and the horse, able to remember the eohippus and foresee the horse, able to see its line of development and promote it, able to invent and teach exercises by which to lengthen its legs and shorten its un-

necessary toes, gladdened by a clear consciousness that it was going to reach the desired goal
and could help itself forward, we get a sort of
parallel to our own position.

But when at last the perception of evolution did
reach mankind, it came to minds already so heavily masculized that they were unable to see this
universal process as one of growth; all they could
see was their own process—combat. "The
struggle for existence" is the popular idea of
evolution. Evolution is what makes an egg
hatch. It does not have to fight with anything,
it just grows. The seed in the earth is no fighter,
but it grows. By simple accretion of particles a
growing root will split a rock, but it does not
fight the rock; "it takes two to make a quarrel."

Growth is the natural law, and the human being adds to growth the new power of culture.

Improvement through heredity is a reproductive process, most powerfully promoted by the
female.

Improvement through culture is a race process,
which has no relation to sex, except as we may
claim it to be a higher extension of work originating in motherhood.

Improvement through combat is a sex process proper to males, by which the victor transmits his superior strength to the young.

On that male tendency to combat, on his instinctive delight in it rests our later doctrine that there is some virtue inherent in effort, that hard things are good for us, that it is not good to make things easy. It is true that at times it is necessary to do difficult things, but not true that their advantage lies in their difficulty.

The natural law is to reduce difficulties, to make every present activity easier in order that we may undertake higher ones, and this is clearly proved in every cultural process. Our wealth and power rest on cultural processes, not on combative ones. By taking care of plant life and animal life we have raised all the food of the world. We develop nothing by combat, unless it is the game-cock, a useless creature kept to amuse men.

Now, if we can see the position of the normal human mother in her responsibility to human life, to human progress, there begins to appear some shining dawn of what the world may expect when she does her duty; some foreshadowing of her effect upon religion, and of the wide new hope which such changed religion would open to us.

First and deepest is the conscious recognition of that great fact of reproduction which is unconsciously submitted to by lower mothers—that life inheres in the race, which is undying, rather than in the individual, which dies. In uncounted millions mothers have bowed to this law, caring nothing for their own lives so that their young might live. This we have foolishly called "the maternal sacrifice." It is not a sacrifice at all; it is a life process, as natural as any other. When the time arrived that the mother was of more use to the young by staying alive, she stayed alive. She, in those early forms, had no more consciousness of virtue or of power than had her mate; but she, human and conscious, can visualize her duty, her first duty as a female, to maintain and to improve the human race.

This she has never recognized until now; still hardly sees.

For all the ages she has been taught that her first, last, and only duty was to man. Her very children were for him; indeed, he fondly supposed that he alone gave them life, she being but the soil in which to plant the seed.   All the laws and all the religious worked to the same end,—that embodied in our Pauline instruction, "Wives submit yourselves to your husbands,"—so she submitted, to our racial degradation; or rebelled, and was destroyed.

The new motherhood will submit to nothing but its own great governing law—to maintain and improve the human race.   It will recognize that its whole duty is to the race through the child, and that all the loveliness of love, all the happiness of kind association, every beautiful higher growth which has come to the relation of the sexes in humanity are subsequent to the primal duty. They assist, promote, and beautify the human sex relation, but they must not contravert its reason for being.   The human mother will see down the ages.   Her children will not end with one generation, nor with two.   She can consciously and effectively build a better race as naturally as some poor insect lays her eggs and dies.   We have not yet had the human mother in her freedom and power, only the subject mother, helpless and oversexed.   In   normal   motherhood,   sex   use will be measured by its service to the young, not its enjoyment by the individual.

In the third chapter was briefly indicated the essential difference in approach of the awakening mind of woman, as religious ideas began to form. From her great function, birth, with its long period of prevision, its climactic expression in bringing forth the child, its years of unselfish service with rich results, she would have apprehended God in a widely different view from that of man—as a power promoting endless growth.

When, now and later, she boldly brings to bear on existing religions this life-based view, this view so wholly in consonance with all the laws we know, and so plainly adapted to bettering human conduct, we may look for large results. It is naturally difficult for us, so long trained in death-based theories, with the concept of a personal God trying to rescue a pitiful few from a ruined world, to face the absolute reverse—the thought of God as a successfully acting power engaged in improving the world, with ourselves as conscious helpers in the process.

In place of cringing away from our responsibility, and shouldering it off on some principle
of evil, some devil, or some woman, we shall
frankly admit that there is nothing the matter
with the world but our own behavior. Able at
last to see what it is that is doing the mischief,
we are able also to stop it.

Our primitive ideas of God, which we insist
on maintaining as immovably as possible, have
left us in strange difficulties as to human
trouble. To a personalized and masculized
deity we attributed all knowledge and all power;
to ourselves we attributed nothing but "poor
human nature"; and then, having to face the
obvious miseries of life, the explanation was
sought in some "inscrutable" purpose of God or
in some malicious anti-god of awful power.
Of late years the somewhat clearer and less rev-
erent mind of man has postulated a god good
enough as far as he went but incomplete; a
young half-grown deity, doing his best with his
world, and likely to improve.

But thought of God aroused by birth leads
along a different road, to a different conclusion.
The primitive woman had no more knowledge

than the primitive man, but she had impulses and feelings quite other than his, and utterly different experiences. Early religion was not built on knowledge but on impulses, feelings, and experiences.

From hers would naturally arise such thoughts as these:

"Here is Life. It comes in installments, not all at once. The old ones die, the new ones come. They do not come ready-made; they are not finished, they have to be taken care of. It is a pleasure to take care of them, to make new people. Everywhere we see the same process, motherhood carrying on life. The mother tree has seeds which make new trees, the mother birds lay eggs which make new birds, the mother beast brings forth her little one to take her place in time and carry on the line. . . .

"What a wonderful thing is Life! Life everlasting, going on continuously, in steps, the ever-coming new ones taking the place of the old worn-out ones—how beautiful! And we cannot stop it if we would; nothing stops it; after the flood has fallen, after the ice is melted, after the forest fire has burnt out, year after year when

winter is over, rises Life, always young, re-born
—how glorious! . . .

"This grain is large and fine, it grows best in
this kind of soil, I will pull out the other things
around so that it will grow better. I will get
some more and plant it here where it grows
best. . . . This seed which I planted and took
care of is better than what grew without help.
I can make things better by takin᷈ care of
them. . . .

"I have taught my child all I knew. He is
wiser than that other whose mother died; who
grew up, indeed, but is not so wise. Teaching
is a help in living. Care and teaching makes
things better. . . .

"I can make things! I can make pots of
clay. I can make baskets of reeds. I can make
clothes of skins. I can build a shelter for my
little ones. I can soften food with fire—it keeps
longer if it is cooked. . . .

"Not only can I make things but I can make
them beautiful! With colors, with stitches, with
lines on the soft clay, with patterns in the woven
reeds, I can make beauty! Beauty! What a
pleasure it is to be skilful and make things, and to

make them beautiful!   I will teach my daughter. . . .

"She has thought of a new pattern, more beautiful than mine.   Ah!   Life is not only in the animals: it is in the things we make; they grow too!   Life, always coming, through motherhood, always growing, always improving through care and teaching!   And this new product of life—not babies but things, useful things, made beautiful—what a joy life is! . . .

"What does it all?   What is behind it all? Who is the first Mother, Teacher, Server, Maker?   What Power under all this pouring flood of Life?   What Love behind this ceaseless mother-love?   What Goodness to make Life so good, so full of growing joy?". . . .

Thus would the woman's mind have reached the thought of God.

CHAPTER XIV

WE have indicated something of the kind of faith which is aroused through conscious motherhood, a faith resting firmly on the laws of nature, seeing God work through them.

What lines of action would naturally follow? In what way would they differ from the action encouraged by previous beliefs?

Primarily and essentially they differ in agreeing with natural impulse instead of undertaking a permanent struggle with it. The natural impulses of motherhood are altruistic in origin, and so tend to develop. The services of motherhood are immediately useful, and tend to become increasingly so. Therefore the growth of conduct would lead on into wider social coördination, without having to struggle with inner impulses of a destructive nature.

That group of impulses which, originally normal and useful, have become so injurious to social growth through long over-development, do not so operate through the mother. Free from the agony of fear, the weight of a looming sense of evil, the constant difficulty of struggling against one's own desires, motherhood's beneficent activities tend to widen into rich and peaceful social relationships. The effect of such a maternal faith, and such natural lines of conduct, upon social economics is clear.

We see about us to-day the widening breach between religion and what we call "Labor," the very recognition of which as a class shows how false is our economic system. "Labor" is the normal functioning of human beings. Any human beings who do not labor are in process of atrophy and decay, are passive as parasites, or are virulent as disease.

Human life consists in the ceaseless, continuous social processes, such as production, distribution, education, government, art, invention. Not to function socially in some useful relationship is not to be human. The economic activities of the mother, beginning in simple maternal instinct, soon assumed group forms and developed group forces.

Language itself, the early requisite of further growth. came through woman's activities, rather than in the solitary efforts of the huntsman. Even where hunting was done in groups, the hunters must be silent lest the prey escape. Hunting, fishing, and fighting do not develop conversation; they are sub-human activities.

Natural growth of organic relation in conscious work, carries with it the essential pleasure of fulfilment. It is more pleasurable to do things together than to do them alone, and far more profitable. So easily and naturally flows the deepening, widening current of our social activities, with satisfaction in the doing and in the results. Here we see personal love and service, personal satisfaction in fulfilment of function becoming that immeasurably greater thing, social love and service, and social satisfaction.

In our previous history such normal growth has been so overlaid by the long oppression of slave labor, so falsified by the arbitrary concepts of reward and punishment, that it is hard for most of us to recognize human work in its true nature.

As religion has followed these same false concepts, its only contribution to the cruel lot of those who carried the world upon their shoulders was the teaching of contentment and the promise of reward when all was done.

Our usual attitude in this matter is very clearly expressed by *The Soul* in Balderstone's "A Morality Play for the Leisure Class":

"Work is trying to do or reach or get something you want. I used to work for money. But whether it's money, a woman, a bird, or a mountain top you're after, you must want what you work for. . . . Nothing to work for, no work."

It is to this underlying misconception, originating in over-indulged desires, crystallized unshakably by ages of slavery, and never contradicted by religion, that we owe the painful phenomena of our "labor troubles."

Absolutely opposite to it is the real source of human work, the love and service of the mother. She works, not to get but to give. She gives, not as a reward but in order to promote growth. From her natural tendencies the applied labor of the world would have been seen, first as a natural expression of energy, secondly as a pleasure in the doing, and thirdly as an increasing benefit to the human race.

The difference is so profound, our present race traditions are so utterly contradictory, that it requires a decided effort of the mind to see what after all is but a plain fact in social economics. Nowhere could the superior force of a concept over a fact be better shown. And nowhere could a difference in concept bring about so swift, so vast, so necessary a change in action.

We cannot say how far a free motherhood, in the past, working side by side with the fathers of the race, would have modified our ideas, but the tendency would have been there, backed by natural law, and saved from the largest errors of our one-sided history. Strongest of all, would have been the help of the life-based religion, practical, natural, joyful, and using its steady strength to keep us true to our normal line of advance.

We cannot reconstruct the past. We can construct a very different future. That future, the future of our children here, needs the immediate strong influence of the human mother, needs the light and hope and power of a religion which any reasonable being can accept. Even an unreasonable being can more easily follow out principles based on law than, as in the past, perpetrate amazing martyrdoms for principles based on nothing at all.

The birth-based religion, constantly revivified by each new life that comes to us, gives no place to sorrow or remorse. The immediate needs of the children who are here leave us no time to lament for the millions of wasted lives behind us. That new sense of human life as one long living stream, which has visibly survived so far, which has reached such heights in real achievement, is itself a foundation for boundless hope and comfort.

Our thronging troubles, when studied in such new light, are seen to be due to mere false attitudes in our minds, false ideas, theories, beliefs. These things do not require centuries for removal. Nothing is more sweepingly sudden than a religious "conversion," or more miraculously productive of changed conduct.

If the conversion is to some theory which is not true, and requires action which is against nature, the results are not permanent. But the tremendous change of base in our religion, from death to birth; from seeing life as a struggle with nature in order to reach another world, to seeing it as a fulfilment of natural law in order to carry on God's work in this one—this change will keep.

Its relief to the strained and struggling soul will be like stepping from a tight-rope to the solid ground.

No swift flood of utter peace is promised. Nothing but an anæsthetic can instantly bring relief to our long-mishandled minds. It will be noticed that some of our most soothing faiths have precisely that deadening effect. The patient no longer suffers, but neither does he do anything else.

The amount of misery we have made for ourselves is not to be waved out of sight by any rational being. A mind which is willing to stop functioning can ignore the world's pain by saying there is n't any, much like the fabled ostrich sticking his head in the sand.

The mother-heart of the world cannot choose but ache for our suffering, but the mother-head of the world can bring new truth to direct our steps in swift relief. Women, in small societies, religious, or charitable, have always tried in a futile, limited way to heal and teach and help the helpless; we see them now in great organizations trailing after destroying armies of men, to nurse the wounded, teach the blind and crippled, rebuild the ruins; trying to apply productive womanhood to offset the evils of destructive men.

So the women of the world, once they realize that their nature is more human than man's, that all this fighting is the result not of human nature but of sex nature, will be able to exercise an unmeasured influence to maintain peace. No peace can ever be maintained in a wholly male world. No war could ever endure for long in a world of equal men and women. But this means real women, normal women, with brother, husband, and son who are normal men.

Feeble-mindedness in children is often found to be caused by bodily defects, and so remediable. Real insanity is often caused by false ideas, as in religious dementia. When we come to analyze our social idiocies and manias on similar lines, we shall find prompt relief. Con-

sistency is a natural function of the mind.   If
the premises are wrong, our best logic only leads
us astray.

The new premises for our religious thought
will as inevitably lead to right conduct as the old
premises have led to wrong.   Where the older
religions left life on earth neglected, the new will
find its place of action here.   Where the old saw
human labor as a curse, the new will find in it
joyful and natural expression of power.   Where
the old demanded belief in the unprovable and
supernatural, the new will develop understanding of clear natural law.   Where the old issued
commands, the new will show cause and effect.
Where the old drove the unwilling by threats of
punishment, or lured them by promise of reward,
the new will cultivate the natural powers which
lead and push us on.   Where the old saw life
as evil and humanity as a broken, feeble thing,
the new will see life as a glory, and humanity as
its highest crown, rich with untested powers.

Our old position, based on a misplaced relationship and buttressed by religions so derived,
makes of this world a place where a pitifully
limited motherhood, itself debased and warped

by long misuse, still does its best in love and service for the child, at home. This child, when grown, must go out into a world which is not a home but a race-course, a fighting-ring with neither ropes nor rules save the always belated struggles of the law, and what we proudly call "the stern arbitrament of the sword." This world is virtually deserted by religion, and shows it. We have been taught how to "renounce the world," and, in various forms of charitable effort, how to assuage its pains somewhat, but not told how to manage it so that it shall be a credit to us and a lovely place to live in.

To the mother's mind this is a self-evident duty—at home. She teaches and practises, as far as she is able, the pleasant virtues and mingled services which make us find "home" the sweetest word we know, and feelingly add, "What is home without a mother?" Precisely the tendencies so working at home will work in the world when this wide, sweeping flood of new conviction shows women at last their long-neglected duty in our common home, the world.

She who feeds her children in order that they may grow, cannot, it is true, in the twinkling of an eye change the masculine view that nothing is to be given until after it has been worked for.

Yet as we see the whole black cloud of evil in the sex relation fade away when the natural pre-eminence and freedom of the mother is recognized and her selective power rightly exerted; as we see war gradually disappear when an international motherhood takes the steps, so clearly possible, to protect the children of the world, so may we see a change in the very foundations of our economic misery and confusion.

It is an essential, a primal duty, of motherhood to provide for the coming race. No bird, beast, or insect mother fails to do her best for the next generation. Even fish and reptiles often make long journey to lay their eggs in places advantageous to the young.

The human mother, as a separate animal, has the same personal instinct, and as a human being has the collective instinct and the collective power to provide in advance for the proper birth and care for all human young. Yet we find in the human race such wide-spread poverty that millions of children are so born, so reared, as to degenerate instead of improving, to die instead of living.

This condition has never been approached by mothers as within their responsibility. Being individually dependent upon their husbands, they were unable to affect their own economic condition, or that of their children; and any sustained objection on their part was promptly quieted by religion with its teaching of contentment, of submission, and of the moral advantages of poverty.

Stationary in their primitive trade of handwork in the home, they never kept pace with the economic development of men, and accepted perforce the explanations vouchsafed by men as to the disasters and deprivations which fell upon them. Minds always narrowed by the petty demands of personal service, taught that they were incapable of understanding "man's work" and taught little else, could not be expected to grasp much of the widening economic processes of the world.

We are so used to the strange aborted position of the house-bound woman, living in the great world as if she were by nature only a servant and a prisoner there, that we do not yet begin to appreciate what the world has lost by losing its mother. She bore children, it is true, else we should not be here; she taught them what she knew, which was not much; but of the world they were to live in she was kept in ignorance, and was unable to improve it.

It is still a new world to her; she is still slow to recognize that the social conditions she finds herself in are not necessarily permanent, wise, or right. Of these conditions the most pressing are those of economics.

The development of social economics, solely in male hands, has been, to say the least, wayward. Since the industrial urge comes through motherhood and was crushed into slavery at an early period; since slavery was a condition wholly consonant with the master's masculine desires, we see the history of labor to be for the most part a history of slave labor. The woman works cheerfully for her children, because it is her nature to. The man, slave-born and pain-driven, worked sadly for his master, because he had to. The serf, last dwindling form of slave, still worked for his lord because he must. The employee, working "for his living," under fear of death if he refuses, is still called "a wage slave." He may change his job if he will,—and if he can find another,—but there is no way of escape save vagrancy, the last resort of the unwilling male worker.

Meanwhile the master, the lord, the owner, the employer, carries on the stimulating old predatory method of getting a living, inherently natural to the male. He was a hunter and fighter for far more ages than he has been a worker. Predatory warfare, piracy, discovery of hidden treasure, exploitation of women's labor and later of men's, the game of finance, have always been easier, more exciting, more attractive to the male of our species than plain work.

Beneath ultra-masculine dominance has feebly grown the normal human delight in work as fulfilment of function, so far felt mainly by those in the higher professions, freely chosen. Its natural enjoyment has been held back by the unnecessary cruelties of enforced labor, and discouraged by the religious teaching that labor was a curse; yet it has grown to such undeniable height as to show us the "martyr to science," and the less conspicuous martyr to duty, as the telephone girl holding her place while the fire draws near.

While production has been thus perverted and retarded, distribution has been so interfered with that whole societies have been checked by its abnormalities, with the majority of the people warped in growth. Yet the "economic problems" which so oppress us, do not seem so complicated when viewed by social motherhood. They are primarily these:

How to produce the most and best to meet our needs, in the least time, with the least effort and expense, the most ease and pleasure; and

How to distribute the product to the most people, in the least time, with the least effort and expense, the most ease and pleasure.

Surely there is nothing insuperable in these! Yet our production is irregular, often inferior or insufficient; while our distribution is so grossly disordered that we find a state of unwholesome congestion among the rich, and a general pernicious anæmia among the poor. Nothing but false religious teaching could uphold so evil a condition as poverty, in a people of measureless potential wealth.   Most theorists who have arisen to protest, seek to substitute some arbitrary system of their own, based on various fallacies, still governed by the masculine impulse to combat, postulating a war between classes, urging hate and violence.   The most conspicuous and ghastly failure of artificial distribution is shown by those who prey on slaughtered Russia.   Their performance is like that of one who has killed some sufferer from diseased circulation, and then set up an extraneous machine to pump the dead blood through dead veins.

Our natural economic processes have been most unnaturally interfered with by the ultra-greed which comes from over-indulgence; the ultra-combativeness which is the inevitable accompaniment of excessive sex; and the false theories of death-based religion and religion-warped education. Man the human creature tends to rise in peaceful enlargement of prosperity and intelligence; but man the male has hindered his own growth at every step.

Debarred from normal joy in fulfilment of function by the system of slave labor, he has frequently reverted to the earlier position of predatory robber, or sunk still further to mere parasitism.   It is as pathetic as it is disastrous to see the rising human spirit, whose normal growth would have been accompanied by general wealth and peace and beauty, so persistently handicapped by its attendant deformity, the spirit of abnormal sex.

We have great names and many to prove the true human spirit, such as Agassiz, who "had not time to make money" because of his joyous devotion to science; Stradivarius, delighting in his master violins; Ruskin, neither poor nor highly sexed, yet working heartily for art and beauty; and besides the great names there are little ones past counting, who choose some ill-paid work, like that of a common sailor, because they care more for the process than for the pay. All the splendid line of inventors, discoverers, artists, teachers, preachers, social servants in all fields, show the irresistible urge, the joy and pride, of normal human work. Against our natural happiness in doing what one is fitted for and therefore loves, we see instead the slow, weary misery of doing under compulsion what one does not like and is not fitted for, with religion solemnly upholding such labor as beneficial to the soul. "Blessed be drudgery!"

Besides this dreary state is another, even more serious—the proportion of social parasites who neither produce nor distribute but creep and crowd over both these functions, sucking from them the social life-blood under the name of "profits." That rich increase of a daily more productive race whose capacities are increased so enormously by machinery and applied power, which should so obviously go back "into the business," the business of race-improvement, has been as far as possible drawn away as fast as it was made, by individuals, and consumed by them in injurious self-indulgence.

The diseased condition has at present become acute in our culture, working to the same destructive ends which we see in the ruined civilizations of the past. Its distresses are still voiced in the old terms, the slave-hatred of labor, the master-contempt for labor, the personal greed of both master and slave. Here is, as ever, the intermasculine struggle, into which it is no wonder men were so unwilling to have women enter.

To the normal woman there is not the faintest need for any "struggle." She knows that every normal child delights to "work" if the work is the kind he likes; and that if he is properly fed and taught and generally comfortable he has strength for exertion and pride in accomplishment. She knows that work is the expression of power, and that power comes from the nourishment one has had, not from what one is going to have.

The whole feminine attitude toward life differs essentially from the masculine, because of her superior adaptation to the service of others, her rich fund of surplus energy for such service. Her philosophy will so differ, her religion must so differ, and her conduct, based on natural impulses, justified by philosophy and ennobled by religion, will change our social economics at the very root.

The elaborate structure of "political economy" with which men have sought to explain and justify their strange behavior, is much like the other elaborate structures evolved from the detached floating theories of speculative religions. To the mother the gross absurdities of food going to waste in one place and children starving in another cannot be explained away by any number of thick books.

The innate, underlying difference is one of principle. On the one hand, the principle of struggle, conflict, competition, the results of which make our "economic problems." On the other, the principle of growth, of culture, of applying service and nourishment in order to produce improvement.

This difference in principle, once expressed in religion, must tend to change our industrial relations for the better.

CHAPTER XV

HOPE AND POWER

THE early Christians expected the world to come to an end at once. They were to be changed in the twinkling of an eye. Under this swift hope they faced death and torture gladly.

The modern evolutionist, looking back at the long ages of previous development, carried on by the slow and wasteful process of "elimination of the unfit," expects no better fate for us, and sees no better method.

How strange it is, how strong a proof again of the force of a concept over a fact, that all our ages of agriculture, horticulture, floriculture, and the rest have not taught us that applied intelligence can speed up evolution! The breeder of animals or the raiser of plants uses natural forces, to be sure, but does not leave his vegetable or animal charges to "struggle" and "survive."

We human beings not only have the same proc-

esses of nature to grow with but add the
social processes, imitation, education, the influence of the whole social environment. Those
who progress beyond the mass have the power to
give their gain to others, a thing no other animal
can do to the same extent. It is true that an
educated elephant can help to tame and teach
one newly caught, but in no species but our own
do "evil communications corrupt good manners"
and good ones improve them, as is seen in human
life.

We shall not be changed into health, beauty,
and rich peace in the twinkling of an eye, neither
do we have to wait for millions of years. Social
evolution can work miracles when it is consciously directed, just as Burbank has worked
miracles in vegetable evolution. We cannot
dictate in our own breeding as if we were cattle,
but a roused social conscience among women can
safeguard and ennoble that process.

A vivid and beautiful instance of woman's
power was shown in the play "A Bill of Divorce-
ment," wherein a modern girl, finding that there
was hereditary insanity in her family, broke with
her lover. She did not offer him a birth-con-

trolled, childless life, but left him free to raise a family; she was a social hero.

But mere selection of the fittest is barely a beginning of what may be done in race-improvement. Most of all we need the constant teaching that this improvement is a religious duty, *the* religious duty above all. Then we have to face a work which has the fascination, the exhilaration, of mountain-climbing. As each new-won height shows us a wider land below and farther heights above, so will this endless path of human progress enlarge our social horizon and open more glorious ambitions before us.

One little stone may turn a baby river to an eastern or a western ocean. A change in human thought like this can turn the course of the world.

The greatest changes in human life are changes in its thought. All the natural facts lay about us for blind ages; they were never ours until we had them in our minds, until we understood them. Each new religion which has come to the world has brought the same kind of foundation, some new vision, some new theory of life. According to its truth it was useful, or, rather, according to our power to accept its truth.

The "newness" of religion here discussed does not involve any contradiction of the previous truths taught in past ages. It does involve the discarding of various beliefs, and the apprehension of some new ones. The new ones offered are not strange to any well-informed modern mind: that evolution means growth, not mere combat; that the human race is young and growing and open to measureless improvement; that the female is the race type and her natural impulses are more in accordance with the laws of growth than those of the male; that the race lives immortally on earth, re-created through birth, and so, through love and service, may rise continually; that social development as a conscious process is our chief duty; that God is the Life within us, the Life of the world, to be worshiped in fruition; that religion is the strongest help in modifying our conscious behavior, but that it cannot so help in social evolution without teaching these truths.

All this we may be able to accept, in that large space of our minds in which we store "beliefs." So held, it will do no more good than do any other of the varied faiths preserved in that museum. The habit of believing a thing, with no result in conduct, is one great evil which we owe to the fixed religions of the past. The hope of the new view is in its essential appeal to nature's main line of applied power, motherhood.

It has been possible for the minds of men to "believe" in Jesus and keep on fighting just the same. Women, so believing, became submissive and obedient. Christianity has been an invaluable religion for women and slaves, as Nietzsche has so violently shown, but this does not carry the reproach he intended. The women and the slaves were higher human types by far than that apotheosis of the male, the "great blond beast" he so extolled.

There is one general hope before the lazy, the weak, the irresponsible, in regard to the coming change of view: namely, that it *is* coming. But whether our own children and grandchildren will be benefited much, depends on us, now; on our immediate conduct. There are two lines of action before us, both indispensable; one in our separate minds, the other in our united conduct. The change in our minds is not altogether easy. After the main position is accepted, there follows a moving of mental furniture as extensive as can well be imagined.

Before those who wish to preach the life-based religion three wide fields are open. There are the "doctrines," large, reliable, provable truths, bringing boundless hope as well as peace and comfort. There are the explanations, applying these truths to show us what has made our troubles in the past and will make our joy in the future. And there is the great new province of social research, now beginning to be studied, that we may learn how most safely, surely, and rapidly to help the world.

Are there in such teaching any disadvantages?

Women are only half the world. What have men to fear, to fight, in such reversal of what they have long held dear?

Nothing, unless a man should fear and fight his mother; there is no one else coming. It is the mother who is rising, whose deep, sweet current of uplifting love is to pour forward into service. The limitation of her love and service to the home has given us our kitchen-economics, our nursery-ethics, our parlor-manners. Her powers freed from those limits, will lift the world.   Our general sentiment about the mother, our underlying worship of the mother will at last be justified when she steps forward into the larger motherhood of the world, her world as much as man's.

The man does lose sex supremacy.   It never belonged to him.   His period of mastership has been marked too blackly with the crimes and diseases of that usurpation, to be regretted.   But he does not lose his race supremacy, a far higher thing.   It will be generations yet before women can cease to depend on men for service, help, and teaching in all the thousand lines of world-service.   Men have made the world, men are the world, in this sense, with room for all the pride they need.   That honest pride in real human accomplishment ought to enable them to bear dissociation of their achievements from their sex.

Why should men dread to face a world more human and less sexual?   Will not the wide and steady increase of human happiness, human beauty, human power, and human love make up to them for the kind of world behind us?   Are men, in truth, so satisfied with the kind of women they have made?   Do they not already

know well the blessing of that human affection
we call friendship, "passing the love of women"?

It is true that life looks dull to them without
its struggling and fighting; but when the morbid
impulse which produces it is no longer felt, the
warfare will not be missed. Moreover, if fighting must be had, there is room for all the furious
energy of every man alive in resisting the relentless grip of the "Dead Hand," the huge, heavy,
driving pressure of the past.

Our natural impulses are good, and need no
harsh suppression, but our unnatural impulses,
the wrong habits of ages, urging us to all manner of evil conduct—these are enemies indeed.
Whoso ruleth his ancestors' spirit is greater than
he that taketh a city.

The highest chivalry ever taught is needed
now to reach the hand of patient helpfulness to
the half-grown woman creature as she strives
toward humanness. The virtues dearest to men
—truth, courage, justice—must be taught to
women. There is before us no overturning, no
attempt at a new domination of women over
men. The woman, acknowledging her back-
wardness, has to face exertion quite outside her

old experience, in the long upward road. She has to grow, to reach his height; man has to wait and help her on. It is not a contest between them, but a recognition of a common hope, a common power, a common duty.

Men are going to lose a servant, a victim, a vampire, a "horse-leech's daughter, crying, 'Give! Give'!" They will gain a woman more worth loving than they have ever known.

If we can assume any large group of people as affected strongly by this new attitude in religion, or scattered small groups here and there, what conduct should be urged upon them? In what respects would it differ from that now practised by progressive thinkers in any religion?

In many respects it would not differ. Every legitimate step toward race-improvement already started could be pushed forward with new hope and new vigor. The world about us is sprouting like a garden in the spring, with all manner of undertakings which tend to help us on. But these, at present, are jumbled without proportion or relation, earnest persons pushing their favored benefit or reform beside or against others, with small knowledge of what it is they are trying to improve.

Charity, that social osmosis by which withheld nutrition has forced its way through diseased tissues of the body politic, still diverts simple minds from such change in industrial relationship as would make all charity needless. And religion, straddling between its old belief that poverty was almost a virtue and its new perception that it is almost a crime, both helps and hinders.

To clarify and relate these efforts we must seek the aid of social experts, as men employ business experts to advise industrial improvements. Sociology is a new study; we have so recently become conscious of our large relationship that it is too soon to look for an established science. But earnest students will find no great difficulty in ascertaining enough gèneral facts, enough proven processes, to begin on.

No one needs special knowledge to see the basic needs of mere physical humanity, as good air, good food, good housing, good clothing, good education, and good employment.

While those who are strongest in study, or in teaching, set themselves to learn the next steps forward, those who prefer action need be at no loss. Whatever lingering ideas of the advantages of difficulty and pain still confuse our minds as to grown men, there is no confusion as to the needs of children. Every step known to improve the health, beauty, intelligence, and right growth of children may be undertaken at once with full assurance of right doing; and every condition which harms them should be at once removed.

With the first glimmer of perception of true social development we should end at once the suicidal folly of "child labor," that utter disgrace to our country. We have some ten million women voters: let them rise to an immediate duty, and end this crime within a year.

Here, as in all our "social problems" we need the religious fervor which has so far been reserved mainly for our private affairs. The inner convictions of the individual, his adherence to this or that creed or article of a creed; his fulfilment of the petty observances required by his particular faith; and the eager efforts of one set of "believers" to make other people "believe" as they do—these have absorbed our religious enthusiasm.

Missionaries the world over find it easier to teach the A, B, C's of their religion to people of some other religion, or without any, than they do to carry out their own religion in their own country.

The life-based kind works differently. Religion is not a private affair. "Believing" it is of no consequence whatever, unless it is applied, and its application requires the continuous behavior of all people for as long as the race endures.

Religion is not a skylight; it is the Front Door.

That supreme engine, the human brain, is supplied with power.

The nature of this power, the amount of this power, we do not understand, and do not need to understand—so that we use it well.

We see in other animals the current of force flowing through them along accustomed channels, in volume which sometimes surprises us.

In the young creature this stream of energy, not yet needed in self-support, expresses itself in "play," in the gay and purposeless practice of actions which will later be carried on in serious earnest.

We are amazed by that rising flood of impulse which stirs in migratory birds, rousing them all at one season to undertake incredible journeys, guided only by that inner urge. Bruce was impressed with the tireless patience of the spider, Solomon with the ceaseless industry of the ant. The driving power which animates a creature is as real a force as the power driving a wind- or water-mill, as steam or electricity.

We, through our larger engine, receive and transmit more power. One steady purpose sometimes animates a man from youth to age; or different purposes engross him, and he fulfills each in turn. Mothers, left alone to rear their children, achieve miracles in labor and self-denial; a wife loving an invalid husband will serve and cherish him to an unbelievable extent. Men, in the service of the women they love, of their country, or of some art or science, again amaze us by the power which maintains their efforts.

This power varies among individuals; some seem to have far more at their command than others. Also, in the same person it varies; a man or woman will seem weak at one time and strong at others. It not only is supplied to each brain separately but may be transmitted from one to another. The person having more power than another and the gift of transmitting it, is known as a "leader," whether it is in the play of children or the work of men.

The brain, as an engine, must be used, to be kept in good working order; and if it is capable of transmitting a thousand volts and used only to transmit fifty, most of it suffers. We have the capacity for transmitting an intensity of power suitable to our degree of human development, but very few of us use it. Those who do, frequently misuse it, spending vast energy in insufficient achievements, as women in the elaborate functions of what they fondly call "society," or men, already rich, working mightily to get richer.

Children, young people not yet at work, and idle grown people, pour out their splendid flow of human energy in amusing themselves; and since this paltry occupation cannot possibly employ the full charge of power, their amusements tend to morbid activities and strange excesses. Among young people denied proper education, proper employment, or the means for amusement, this stream of power often expresses itself in those abnormal enterprises which we call criminal.

Those thinkers who have begun to be conscious of the vast powers which are at the command of the human brain have not, so far, used them to the best advantage. The highly developed brains of China have been used mainly in ceaseless study of Chinese classics, and the practice of ancient Chinese philosophy. The thinkers of India, second to none in power, spend it inside their brains, as it were, thinking without doing. In what we term the more progressive races, much energy is spent in different lines of work, in scientific research, in noble efforts to benefit humanity in various lines. Any one undertaking some special line of social therapeutics soon finds others running parallel or counter to it, and feels the need of coördination, as in "The United Charities." The "push" of the world is largely dissipated.

Nothing gives such exalted pleasure to the human consciousness as to feel the full tide of energy flowing through it. In children we call this "excitement," and rather blame them for wanting it. Hard-working people, which means almost everybody, are too tired of doing one thing all day to have much energy left for anything else; yet in youth the laborer will cap a day's work with an evening's amusement, and feel the better for it. One may be tired to the point of exhaustion by doing something which never calls for one's full power. This is shown most keenly in the evil of long hours spent in ultra-specialized industry.

The greatest delight is felt when one's full power is used in some activity which is believed to be of the greatest value to mankind. Without that expression, there is still pleasure in the mere sensation of the flood of energy pouring through; as in a mighty ambition, or a deep love. Even hate, and grief, as forms of energy, have their attractions. We like to "feel," and feeling must be either in force coming in or in force going out.

What most mars human happiness, even where the ordinary basic comforts and pleasures of life are attained, is the confusion, the interruption, the misdirection, sometimes the complete blocking of the flood of power. Here is where religion, in that attitude of mind called "worship," has offered us a "spill-way," a channel for discharge of energy in emotion. Men have poured theirs in various forms of ambition and desire, women theirs in devotion to man, or child, or "cause." Perhaps the happiest are those men whose trained abilities are fully used in some art or science which is of visible social value.

For this great current is social, not individual. No possible occupation of an individual living alone on an island, could use that aching pressure of social force; that super-personal energy, developed by and belonging to society. No Don Juan with a hundred harems could satisfy it.

The inner change resultant from the recasting of religious and family relationships, as herein suggested, has deep significance in giving new direction to our channels of power, to our purposes and lines of expression. It involves a new orientation, a different attitude toward life and toward one another.

As we are now, the general arrangement is somewhat like this: In the man's scheme of life he has in the background his religious theory, explaining things after a fashion, and holding out hopes of ultimate satisfaction in regard to much that is confusing now; he has his duty to the state, which may reach heights of noble patriotism; he has his work, through which he fulfils his natural abilities to some extent, by which he supports himself, his wife and family, and in which he finds opportunity to get ahead of other men. The woman he views as "his." She is his relative or some other man's relative. She is a good woman or a bad woman according to her relation to men. She stands highest and dearest as his mother, so valued because of her tireless loving service to him. The child he views as his child, or some other man's child, to be loved, cared for, and disciplined, to be valued in relation to its dutiful behavior and as it contributes to the family pride. If it goes wrong, the father has always held the right to repudiate it, crying, "You are no longer a child of mine," casting it out, or cutting it off with a shilling.

In the woman's scheme of life she shares the religion of the man, usually finding it easier to practise in her field than he does in his. As to her work, until recently she had none except the general housework, nursing, baby-culture, and so on, which all women were expected to carry on by instinct and rule of thumb. To-day she is torn between old duties and new ambitions, with much confusion, suffering, and nervous strain.

As to the state, she is only now entering upon any consciousness of her relationship to it, and can hardly be judged, save in so far as her intentions are visibly for the good of the world even when unwisely expressed. Men she has seen either in direct personal relation, as they have seen her, or in wholly impersonal social re-relation, as workers of all sorts, as they have not learned to see her. A man would notice the personal attractions of a shop-girl or a parlor-maid, where a woman would not similarly be impressed

by the plumber or the milkman. As members
of society, more efficient and experienced than
herself, woman respects men as human beings,
and depends upon them for advice and service to
an extent which ought to satisfy their pride even
when they are not so highly rated as a sex. The
child she views as hers, utterly. She resents the
wisest advice as inferior to her "divine instinct,"
and scoffs at the idea of "expert child-care."
When she does consider the rest of the world, it
is with the same divine instinct, the inborn desire to serve and benefit, but not yet with much
knowledge of methods.

As to the child's attitude toward life, that is
first decided by his home, or we might say by his
kitchen. Most people are too poor to keep servants, most mothers spend their days mainly in the
kitchen, most children grow up with the unavoidable conviction that the principal business of life
is to get dinner. Their early impressions of religion are rather gloomy, and school is to most
of them a sentence of confinement with hard labor. All the opening social emotions are rigidly
kept inside the lines of family, school, and such
"company manners" as are habitual among their

class. When children feel the larger push of power, the need of full expression, this is called love of excitement; they are suppressed and told that they will "settle down" later on.   They do. Our present-day youth often refuses to settle down, but does not rise up.

It is to social *relationship* that the life-based religion brings a vital change.   By the new alignment, the new attitude of humanity toward God, of men toward women, of women toward men, of both toward the child, of the child toward them, and of every one of us toward society, we attain a position which allows free transmission of power.

Seeing God as within us, to be expressed, instead of above us, to be worshipped, is enough to change heaven and earth in our minds, and gradually to bring heaven on earth by our actions.   Seeing human life as one unbroken line, visibly immortal, readily improvable, takes off the weight of discouraged ages, sets us on the broad, bright upward road.   No strait and narrow path, like a turnstile into a park, to squeeze into heaven by,—each for himself and the devil take the hindmost,—but an open way, always broadening as we grow, up which we can help one another.

Men will hold all that they have gained, be praised for all the great, good things that they have done, stand foremost as world-servants for generations yet, but they will learn another view of sex: "As a human I stand highest of all life on earth, a member of society; as a male I am to assist the female in her great work of lifting life." The new view of God brings a sense of boundless hope and power; so the new view of woman will change life utterly. Man will see her not as "his" but as a fellow-creature, strong, noble, free, competent in social service. The domestic subordinate, the too-concentrated and servile wife and mother will rise and rise in his mind, to her true place, a wife far more a friend, a mother not measured by devotion to one's self but as the chief channel of social improvement.

Women will change still more. They have farther to go, and the widening life before them is as an open garden after a closed room. In their hearts will rise the new sense of God, the new measurement of men, the new duty to the world.

What is now called "girlhood," which is accepted as a period for light amusements, and, too often, for a partial promiscuity in the preliminary stages of sex dalliance, will become a time as devout as the novitiate of a nun, as glorious as the training of a queen. The nobility and supreme power of world-motherhood is not fitly approached by years of infantile irresponsibility.

But to the child will come the greatest change. Let us look back at our own youth, our deep questions met with such shallow answers; our longing for "something to happen," for relief from the petty restrictions of a kitchen-based, parlor-bounded family life; our sense of rising power, immense power, with vague desire to do great things, met with good-natured laughter or harsh ridicule and turned back into the arbitrary limits of school life; our puzzlement over confusing rules of behavior, met with the requirement of obedience and faith.

Each new generation brings to the world its highest step in development, the latest, clearest mind, the widest vision—or should do so. Each generation, pushing upward through the primitive confusions of nursery-ethics, harassed by the tri-daily insistence on "table-manners" and less frequent but equally arbitrary "company manners," tormented as to clothes, and dumbly bewildered about the behavior of the "grown-ups," has found in religion a dark mystery, instead of a great light.

Of social relationship the child hears little. His mother has none, his father's is mainly in "politics," concerning which, if questioned, he has to offer the opinions of one "party." The child of the ages, the child of the world, finds himself treated wholly as the child of the family, and is never given a glimpse of his true relation to life.

A misused, subordinate mother gives us an underrated, mistaught child. The world-mother, looking at the child with new eyes, studying as the greatest of social duties the science of child-culture, will give the world at last the full benefit of youth. And youth, at last, will find life opened before it, simple and clear, broad and bright, with a glorious array of things to do, and the conscious flood of power to do them.

We hear much of "youth" to-day, youth which

shows a behavior of premature misguided age. As an old man, acting foolishly, is said to be in his "second childhood," so do these young people, acting foolishly, manifest only a sort of precocious senility.

The spirit of youth is progress, not the imitation of primitive habits of which even old persons are often ashamed. That real spirit, the best hope of the world, when it recognizes that religion is useful, simple, and applicable at once, will drop its playthings and set to work.

There is no need to specify among the wants of humanity.

Taking care of human beings is no mystery. Developing the best abilities of every child is no mystery. What is needed by one family can easily be extended to all, with difference according to individual capacity. We know now plenty of things needed by the world, and can learn more as fast as we accomplish these. It is not direction in detail which the world wants most; it is the broad light of clear duty, the hope of an assured future built by our own hands, growing better with cumulative speed as each generation improves on the work of its predecessors. We need to see and use the power to carry on this racial task, this natural task, this task which is no struggle against our own impulses and desires but the fulfilment of those essentially distinctive of our race.   We need the joy which no creature can possess without the utmost expression of power; which will be ours in increasing measure as we broaden out into full human consciousness and the exercise of the full range of human faculties.

Each of us, once grasping the full sense of a God that works, of our natural relationship to that power being simply fulfilment, the carrying out of our natural race-development, may draw a long breath and take hold in earnest.   Such power is not "angry."   One does not have to apologize to God for every foolishness, any more than a tree apologizes to the sun for worm-eaten apples.

This naturally possessed power is not a mere private medicine-chest, as some seem to think; our world needs much more than healing.   Well people sometimes behave worse than the sick ones.   The power of God is building the world, through us; our place is to see it, use it, rejoice in it. A child has an instinctive longing for happiness, more happiness, always happiness. The child is right. Happiness is our racial right, our racial duty. When we have dismissed from our minds forever the mistakes of our ancestors, outgrown our present deformities and deficiencies, forgotten our unnatural bad habits, and developed natural good ones, happiness will come easier to us. The satisfaction of desire is not happiness, any more than having breakfast. All right and natural desires should be satisfied, of course—in order that we may get to work.

Happiness is fulfilment of function. It is conscious transmission of power. It is the expression of God. It belongs to humanity in a higher degree than to any soaring lark, because we are able to express more God more fully than any other creature.

After a little, a few centuries or so, when we have cleared off all the rubbish from our minds; when the practical lifting of the world is well under way; when health is universal and all of us at the work we love best; when general education has given to every mind its background of common knowledge, its foreground of common hope, then the child's instinct for happiness will be fulfilled.

A glorious ritual of such triumphant religion would be in the glad welcome of each new day. Unwearied people, rising from full sleep, plunging into clean water, clothed in fair apparel, greeting the sun with song. As the advancing wave of sunrise rolled round the earth, so would the advancing wave of music, giving to every soul fresh joy, fresh hope, fresh power.

GIVE WAY!

Shall we not open the human heart,
Swing the doors till the hinges start,
  Stop our worrying doubt- and din,
  Hunting heaven and dodging sin?
There is no need to search so wide;
Open the door and stand aside—
      Let God in!

Shall we not open the human heart
To loving labor in field and mart,
  Working together for all about,
  The glad large labor that knows not doubt?
Can He be held by our narrow rim?

Do the work that is work for Him—
Let God out!

Shall we not open the human heart,
Never to close and stand apart;
  God is a force to give way to!
  God is a thing you have to do!
God can never be caught by prayer,
Hid in your heart and fastened there—
Let God through!